I Remember When

Lincoln Was Shot

I Remember When Lincoln Was Shot

❧

A Memoir by
Justine Klomann Hildebrandt
(1861–1942)

by
Justine Klomann Hildebrandt

Edited by
Anne Walker

Little Miami Publishing Co.
Milford, Ohio
2021

Little Miami Publishing Co.
P.O. Box 588
Milford, Ohio 45150-0588
www.littlemiamibooks.com

Printed in the United States of America on acid-free paper.

ISBN-13: 978-1-941083-26-0

Library of Congress Control Number: 2020948128

Dedication

This memoir is dedicated to Justine's
descendants

—especially my niece, Chloe—

the daughter of the daughter of the
daughter of the daughter of Justine.

Contents

Foreword

JUSTINE KLOMANN HILDEBRANDT was born on October 31, 1861, in rural Ohio outside of Cincinnati. She died on May 3, 1942. She married John Joachim Hildebrandt in about 1881. They had six children, one of whom died in childhood.

My great-grandmother wrote this memoir when she was in her late seventies, in the late 1930s. It covers the period from her earliest memories at four years old, in 1865, through her young adulthood, interspersed with observations from her later life. It is the story of farm and family life in southwestern Ohio.

The manuscript was handwritten on three hundred sheets of five-by-eight-inch plain stationery in a lovely hand. It was stored in a pink stationery box. Her daughter Mary Hildebrandt became the custodian of the memoir until she passed it on to her niece, my mother, Margaret Hildebrandt Avey Walker.

Justine did not complete a formal high school education.

Her writing is often in stream-of-consciousness style with little punctuation and inconsistent spelling. I first transcribed the pages exactly as written and retained a copy of the original version. The pages were unbound, so I sorted them into chapters as I did not know the order in which they were written. My husband, Richard Krohn, then helped me create this edited version which retains Justine's exact words, but corrects spelling and adds punctuation so the reader can enjoy her stories without distraction.

We deposited the original manuscript in the Cincinnati Museum Center at Union Terminal in October 2015, where it is available for research purposes.

I will leave you the pleasure of discovering everything else about Justine in these pages.

Anne Walker
September 15, 2020

Justine Klomann Hildebrandt's Matriline
from maternal grandmother to great granddaughter plus known siblings

Generation 1
- 3 brothers
- Salome (sister)
- **Elizabeth Flickinger Aufranc** 1807-1896

Generation 2
- Louise — B: 1834, D: ?
- Mary — B: 1837, D: ?
- **Elizabeth Aufranc Klomann** 1838-1892
- Augustus — B: 1840, D: ?
- Esther — B: 1843, D: ?
- Magdalene — B: 1846, D: 1879
- Sarah — B: 1848, D: ?
- Amelia — B: 1850, D: 1873

Generation 3
- Clara — B: 1858, D: 1935
- Anthony — B: 1860, D: 1926
- **Justine Klomann Hildebrandt** 1861-1942
- Elizabeth — B: 1863, D: 1943
- Augustus — B: 1865, D: 1934
- Winona — B: 1868, D: 1951
- Emma — B: 1871, D: 1968
- Ernest — B: 1873, D: 1878
- Eva — B: 1879, D: 1962

Generation 4
- Wilhelmina — B: 1882, D: 1894
- Carl — B: 1884, D: 1976
- **Naomi May Hildebrandt Avey** 1887-1936
- Clara — B: 1889, D: 1964
- Mary — B: 1897, D: 1985
- John — B: 1900, D: 1980

Generation 5
- **Margaret H. Avey Walker** 1922-2019

Generation 6
- David — B: 1950, D: 2006
- Steven — B: 1952, D: -
- **Anne Elizabeth Walker** 1954-
- Ellen — B: 1956, D: -
- Carol — B: 1962, D: -

Chapter I

The Klomann Family

My earliest memories

MY MEMORY GOES BACK TO BEFORE I WAS FOUR YEARS OLD.
One of the most vivid incidents is when President Lincoln was
assassinated. I was then four years old and can distinctly remember what a sensation it caused. He was loved by many. But there
were some here in the North that did not think so well of him.
They thought him to blame for so much sorrow and trouble, and
thought it could have been avoided. Even some people in the
North did not think it necessary to free the slaves. It seems too
bad that a great man has to die before it is realized how great a
man he was. After all these years Lincoln is more honored than
he was at that time. I remember the day when he was assassinated. My brother was six and I was four. We climbed up in a
wagon and shouted "Hurrah for Lincoln!" Booth shot him. It
was indeed a sad time for many or most of the people. I do not

remember what difference in the condition of the country it made. I was too young to know anything about that.

My father had a family of a wife and four small children, so he did not have to go and fight. But the war was felt at home even if some were not on the battlefield. Mother would tell us what a hard time my family had while the war lasted. I can remember my mother telling how frightened they were when the Morgan men [Confederate army raiders, summer of 1863] went throughout the country and stole and raided everywhere and took whatever they wanted. She told us how Father drove his matched team of black mares, Coly and Lory, in the woods to hide them. They were valuable and he was very proud of them. I remember them. Father had them many years after the war was over. He would carry the bags of grain and hide them in the loft of the house. They would hide everything that they thought the raiders could carry off in those days. There were many acres of woods, and they thought that the raiders would not take the trouble to go there as they went through. They kept mostly on the highway. One time they unhitched the horses from a hearse in a funeral procession and left their faded horses behind. There were many dreadful things they did. Our mother told us about them. It was hard for anyone to forget. And they say it was even worse in the South. There were so many fine homes ruined there that caused sorrow and heartache.

The war being so near to home, it affected everyone. Prices were so high for all domestic goods as well as food. Mother told us how hard it was to get coffee. She would roast or brown grain such as barley, and mix it with a little real coffee. I can remember some of that. When it was browned and ground (every house owned a coffee and spice grinder in those days), with cream and sugar when they could get it, it was not so bad and I think more wholesome than strong coffee.

All goods for wearing apparel [were] very high. Mother would tell me what a hard time she had to get material to make clothes for a new baby, which was me. She said that muslin was ninety cents a yard and all cotton goods [were] so high that she did not have many changes for me. Of course one can imagine how hard it was to keep anyone much less a baby clean enough to be healthy. For better dresses there were Lustre and Alpaca. I remember my mother's dresses were made of that material. The ladies' riding habits were made of that material, too.

It was like all wars. It left marks of it for many years to come. We knew men with one leg gone and some minus an arm or other wounds that caused them to be cripples and unable to make a living for themselves and families. One such was a grocery keeper where we bought our groceries and sold him our butter and eggs in exchange for groceries. He also drove a huckster wagon through the county and gathered up a load of poultry and calves and butter and eggs. He drove a strong team of mules. He would take a load of such to market every week. He was a man of high temper and well able to take care of himself in spite of the missing leg. He would use his crutch for a weapon as well as helping himself to get around.

Grandmother

My earliest memory of my grandmother was when she lived with three of her daughters, they being the youngest of her eight children: seven girls and one boy. First came Louise, then Mary Justine, Elizabeth (my mother). Then Uncle Augustus [Gus], Esther, Magdalene, Sarah, and the youngest, Amelia. My uncle, Mother's only brother, had gone to a home of his own, his farm adjoining Grandma. Grandmother was a neat little roly-poly French woman who came to this country with her mother and brothers and one sister. I do not remember my grandfather. He passed away when I was two years old.

They lived in a long, low log house such as were many of them in those days. It had two large rooms and a large kitchen built like a lean-to. There was also a loft which they had to climb a ladder to get to. It had a porch which extended clear across the front of the house. It had two long settees, one with a green back and arms, and one just a bench scoured until the wood was almost white. We little children would like to race up and down the porch.

Grandmother was not only a good housekeeper but very neat about herself. For everyday she wore a white ruffled cap and a kerchief, for dress a black lace cap and cape. She wore very full skirts with a huge pocket in them where she carried her belongings. A dress without a pocket in those days was not complete. She always had sugar kisses for us that she carried in her pocket. She would give us one apiece. Sometimes they would be what we called in those days French kisses. They were wrapped in bright fringed papers twisted at each end with a verse wrapped in them. They were for special occasions. She always had something to give us when we went to see her or when she came to visit us. I think that we appreciated that as much as children now days would a whole bag full. We did not expect any more so were satisfied.

She was very orderly and economical, some said stingy, yet she was generous with her food. She also was a very good cook and had many French ways with her cooking. We children would love to visit her. Her bread and cookies and coffee cake were the best. She also was a fine hand in making cheese and butter. Whenever we went to visit she would take us to her well kept cellar and give us something to eat—cookies, bread and butter, and rhubarb jam. I have never forgotten the good bread she baked and how good it tasted to husky youngsters.

After Uncle Gus was married and lived on an adjoining farm he still farmed her land. They later tore down the old log house and built a nice new frame house near where the old one stood. So the well was near. But the spring house had to be done away with. It was in the way for making a nice front yard. She and Aunt Maggie were very fond of flowers. Her garden had a neat white paling fence, and a neat row of flowers separated the vegetables planted in small beds such as lettuce, onions, radishes, beets, carrots, and parsnips. On the other side she would have her potatoes and turnips, beans, and peas, and some other things that needed more room. Everything was done in an orderly way. She also kept two cows and a lot of chickens. All those things, with some fruit trees and currants and gooseberries and rhubarb, supplied them with most of their living.

Their horses and cows and dog had French names. They had one horse, Mignon, one, Cassock, another, Belle. Their cows were Bluehmy and Cheree. Their dogs were Fidele and Bonni. Fidele was a large mastiff and a very good watch dog. But she was not friendly with children, so we were taught not to try to play with her. Grandma would bake cornbread and make mush for them. They always looked sleek and well fed. [They] would lie on one end of the porch. We children were cautioned not to bother the largest one of them. Fidele was a very fine dog and a protection to my grandmother and aunts [but] she was not used to small children and would stand for no petting. No stranger could come on the porch if Grandmother was not there to tell her that it was all right. Such was their watchfulness. She was well named.

Grandma would tell us about their trip here from Alsace Lorraine, which was French when they lived over there. But they were at war with the Germans even then. She came over here with her mother and sister and one brother and his wife.

One brother had been killed in the war. She was eleven years old when they came over, the youngest of the family. Their language was French although she could speak German. But she never did among themselves. She told about the hard trip they had coming over. They came on a sailing vessel and it took them eighteen weeks to get here. Some days they would be going back when the wind came in the wrong direction for them to proceed. Her brother's wife died on the way over, and the sharks were so bad they followed the vessel until they had to bury the body in the sea. They sewed it up in a sheet and threw it overboard. What a terrible thing to do.

[Grandmother] would tell us many interesting stories of her life, the way she came to New Orleans, where there were many other French people. She told how she helped to nurse through a yellow fever epidemic and cholera, too. She never took it. She was not afraid. Her mother died shortly after they came over. So that left her with one brother and her older sister. Her brother died with yellow fever, which was very bad at that time.

Shortly after they arrived they met two young French men that had been here some time. These young men saw their sad plight and befriended them all they could. Grandmother would tell how kind they were. When Grandma was fifteen she married one of the brothers and after they were married eleven years they began to raise a family. She had seven girls and one boy. All lived to be grown up and all but two married, so there were a number of grandchildren. She also would tell us about the experience my grandfather had with Negro slaves and the war that was being fought at that time.

Some years after they were married Grandfather's brother lost his health so they thought they would seek a healthier climate. So they came and started farming near Blue Ash, Ohio. Mother was born there. The brother passed away and was buried in the cemetery there. Grandfather was fond of fine horses and knew much about how to take care of them. He later brought a farm near Tylersville and brought up their family there. Grandfather was some years older than Grandmother and passed away many years before she did.

One word from Grandmother was law. In those days children were taught to obey so we did not get into any trouble. Grandmother later built a new frame house near the old log, so the old house was torn down, and the old spring house where Grandma kept her milk and butter in the summertime. It was like a cave. It had a spring in it and small stream of water ran through it. It was delightful[ly] cool in the summer. The well served for the new house. But in order to have a nice yard the milk house had to be done away with. I do not remember what was done about the spring. It probably found an outlet somewhere else. There were several wells on the place.

Their new house was very nice but we liked the roomy old one. We enjoyed going to Grandma's and went there quite often. Father would hitch up the horses to the spring wagon on Sunday sometimes and take the whole family, which was quite a load. I think there was more visiting done among families and friends than there is in these times. Families seemed very near to each other and more ready to help each other when help was needed.

Later Aunt Sarah was married and gone to a home of her own and Aunt Amelia died. So that left Grandma with Aunt Maggie, who lost her health and was an invalid for a long time. That was hard on Grandma. Sister Lizzie or I would go and stay with her when our Mother could spare us. After Aunt Maggie passed away, Grandma went to live with my uncle. He had taken over her farm so he thought she should stay with them. Grandmother lived longer than mother did.

When she passed away uncle got the farm. It did not seem right to the rest of the heirs. It seemed too much for him to ask for keeping Grandma for such a short time. We knew how our mother would have seen how unjust it was for him to demand so much. It was a good farm with good buildings on it and he had the use of it all the time that Grandma lived. When the settlement was made there was very little for the rest of the rightful heirs. His son seems to have inherited the same tendencies.

Grandmother never liked for us to speak anything but French to her. She would scold us if we spoke English to her although she spoke English very well. She did not want us to forget our French. So we all spoke French while we were very young. We spoke French to Mother and German to Father. We older children could speak French, English and some German. It made little difference which language we used. But when we heard Father and Mother talking English together we soon liked that much better and soon it was that [English] when we talked to each other. Of course after we were old enough to go to school we only used English with each other. People that came to our home and heard us speaking the three languages wondered if we did not get all mixed up. But we managed it very well. My youngest sister never learned the French or German language. By that time we were using the English language and fast forgetting the others. I and some of my sisters can still converse with each other and it is very convenient sometimes.

The only reading we knew in French was when mother would get out an old French Bible she kept in the top drawer of a high chest of drawers we called a bureau where she kept a few other treasures that we were interested in. She would read to us sometimes. I never learned to read very well but I knew some French words when I came across them in my reading, so that was a help to understand what they were. The German was about the same. We could understand when it was read to us and by hearing the men that father hired to work for us. Sometimes they could speak little English and my father would have to talk German to them to make them understand what they were to do.

We also had German neighbors. One woman could not speak English at all and did not seem to learn it. So if we had to talk to her it had to be German or not at all. I managed pretty well with all three languages and so did my oldest sister and brother. We never heard French spoken after Grandmother passed away, and there were no French people around, so it was easy to get out of the habit of using French at any time. If we could have learned to read and write it better we would not have forgotten it so soon. After we heard very little German spoken often enough to hear it where we lived, we got completely out of the habit and forgot most of that, too.

One thing that made a lasting impression on me was [when] Aunt Maggie was sick and I was staying with them to help Grandma. I was then about thirteen. I slept upstairs alone, and one window opened where I could see the woods across a field. Grandmother had a neighbor that had lost a son in the Civil War, and it had unbalanced her mind. She would get out in the middle of the night and call her son. The sound of her voice in the dark saying "Amos, come home!" over and over again—I could hear it plainly and it sounded so terrible.

Needless to say, I could not sleep. I would get up and close the window even if it was very warm and I could still hear her calling "Oh, Amos!" Some said that she carried a knife for her own protection. But I do not think that was true. Her good and faithful husband would follow her, unbeknownst to her, to protect her from harm. She had one daughter that later also lost her mind. One time father sent me on an errand to their house. I went shivering. She did not say a word to me but gave me what

I asked for. It was a half bushel measure. Father wanted it to measure some grain and he had not brought his own with him. I remember the strings of sliced apples she had drying in front of the fireplace. That was one way of doing that in those days. The poor woman was harmless and grief-stricken.

Another thing I remember was Grandma's huge four-poster beds, high enough so they could push a trundle bed under in the daytime. The bedsteads had high posts that almost touched the ceiling and banions around the sides to hide the trundle beds in the day time. Another thing that I remember was the beautiful rosewood clock. It was handmade. Even the works inside were handmade of wood. Its striking sound was very sweet. Grandma always had a certain time to wind it, at six o'clock in the evening. She took care of it herself whenever she was at home.

Another thing was the pictures on the wall. One was a picture of Lincoln and some were pictures of William Tell. Grandfather came from the border of France in Switzerland, and William Tell was his hero like he was to those that came from that country. Grandfather spoke five languages, mostly French, Spanish, Italian, German, and English. My grandmother had a large conch shell. She could play quite a tune on it. We children would like to play with it when we went to visit her. She also used it for a door stop. It seems like she had so many things to interest us. But it did not take so much to amuse us. The big out-of-doors had enough to keep us busy. We had our play houses and our Chinese dolls. We would make our furniture for our play houses such as chairs and bedsteads from corn stalks, and our dishes would be broken pieces of some colored china.

Our pie pans would be any little tin lid we could find. We liked making mud pies. We would pattern them after our mother's. And to this day, seventy-five years [later], I am using the same leaf on the pies that I bake, a habit that has not changed. No improvement you will think for these rushing times. But I have found none that I liked better. And like mother I have made many pies in my long life. Pies used to be our most popular desert. Of course, fruit pies were the most kind we baked. But there were also the custard pies and the vinegar pies. Mother was an expert in making custard pies. I made many of them, too, while I lived in the country. But I do not think I could do as well as she did with them. We would make them and the vinegar pies with raisins in them when food was scarce.

Our family

Our family consisted of six girls and three boys. The eldest was Clara, then Anthony, Justine—myself, Elizabeth, Augustus, Winona, Emma, Ernest, and Eva, five years younger than Ernest. He passed away before Eva was born. So there were eight of us who grew up to man- and womanhood. When I was seventeen and Eva was seven weeks, Sister Clara was married and had two children of her own, so that left seven of us at home. A family of nine people [was] a lot to cook, bake, and wash and iron for, so it kept us all busy. But the boys were old enough, so Father did not have to hire a steady hand to work for us. He would hire men by the day to help out in the busiest times. We were glad when we did not have extra men around. It made cooking more simple so it did not seem so hard.

My mother was a very good cook. And she fed her family very well. We always had plenty of good food, mostly produced on the farm and by my mother's skill. I often wonder how she ever did accomplish so much work. We were nine children, and before my brothers were old enough to help with the farm work my father would hire two steady hands and others at harvest time. So that made more people to feed. And everything had to be gathered and prepared for the cooking. It was not like now.

We could not buy prepared food. We bought our coffee green, and had to roast it and then grind it ourselves. I can remember how we had to watch the coffee so it would not get too brown or overdone so we did not spoil a batch of it. It had to be done very carefully. But it was fresh and made a very good drink.

This is about the babies of our family. I remember the baby that came to our family was Brother Augustus, Gus for short. He was four years younger than I. I remember well the day before he was born we butchered a beef. It had gotten pretty excited and my mother helped to fasten it to a tree. It did not seem to be frightened of her, so they called on her to calm it down. Our cattle, especially the cows, liked my mother and she could handle a nervous cow much better than the men folks could. She would always have to break a young heifer for her first milking. By that time she would have taught them not to be afraid of her by petting them. So when the time came for their first time to be milked they would not be afraid.

Well, the next day little brother arrived. I was a very happy little girl. But I do not remember how my mother got along with all the work and a little new baby. Of course she had help but there were so many things to be looked after, and I do not remember how it was done. In two years after Gus was born, Sister Winona was born. They had sent me to Grandma's to be out of the way. They must have thought that it would be better. I did not mind staying at Grandma's, but when I heard that there was a new baby at home, I wanted to be there, too. My Aunt Maggie was staying with my mother, so she came for me and I was very glad to get home. Little sister became somewhat my charge. I was then six, old enough to help to take care of her. I remember how I tugged her around and would be frightened when I let her fall or fell down with her. But she survived the bumps, and no ill effect came from them.

Next in three years after, late in May, little blond Emma came. I was then old enough and strong enough to be more help to my busy mother. Sister Lizzie, two years younger than I, was able to help look after the baby, too. I remember that she was born one Sunday night so near midnight that they never were sure what date was her birthday. But Mother knew. She must have been the least excited. She said that she looked at the clock so she knew. We had sheared our sheep the week before and father had planned to haul the wool to the woolen mill on Monday and I was going with him, so when I heard the excitement downstairs I thought it was time to get up and get ready. I heard my mother tell my father to make me go back to bed, so I went. I always was a light sleeper and did not have to be called more than once or not even that when it was time to be up and get busy. So it never was a hardship for me to get up early. I would get up to help mother get breakfast and learned to bake pancakes when I was quite young.

Just two years after Emmy was born, little Ernest came. That was the time we all had the whooping cough. And what a time my poor mother had at such a busy time of the year, and a little sick baby and a house full of coughing children. I often wonder how she got through it all. There were no more babies until five years later, Little Eva came. She was a delicate little girl and needed much care. But I was then sixteen and could be more help to my mother. Our oldest sister Clara was married and had two children of her own. I had stayed with her when her youngest little Bertha came, so by the time Eva came I had learned how and could help take care of her. And I know how mother did appreciate my help. I never resented the babies coming. I knew when little Eva was coming. What I did not know, Clara told me, so I had made up my mind that I was going to do all that I could to help mother. I remember scolding Brother

Tony for saying that we did not need the little baby. But he loved her as well as the rest of us did. And how he would tease and teach her to say things to make everyone laugh. Sometimes they were something that little girls should not say and he would get a scolding for it.

Brother Tony was that kind of a boy [that] when he wanted to find out anything, he would go himself and most always get what he went for. One time there was a murder committed in West Chester and there was an inquest to be held on the body [by] the coroner or whoever it was at that time about seventy years ago. Tony knew that our uncle, Aunt Mary's husband, would be there as a witness or something, I do not recall just what. The inquest, as they called a postmortem at that time, was held in the vault of the cemetery. So Tony was there on time. I wonder that they allowed a boy of his age around. Anyway, he saw all that they did at such an occasion. He came home and told us all about the gruesome affair.

Another place where he got a lot of information was at the blacksmith shop. Father would send him with a horse to be shod or a plowshare to be sharpened. There would be men there for the same purpose, so it was a good place to hear plenty of gossip. Things would be talked about that it would have been better for a boy not to hear. But the stories about the war and other things also were interesting to a boy. It did not seem to hurt Tony, and he got a lot of information on different subjects. He knew pretty well when anything he heard should not be repeated.

Brother Gus was six years younger than Tony, but they were very chummy and played and worked together. Gus was a hard worker and began quite young to hold up his end. He tried hard to keep up with Tony. One day they were practicing to see who could hit a fence post the most times. They were both good at throwing straight. Gus hit the post so hard that the stone bounced back and hit Tony in the mouth and broke one of his front teeth off. It grieved Mother so much. Tony had good strong teeth but it was not long until the tooth gave him trouble and had to be taken care of.

We children were a healthy lot and needed little medicine. We scarcely ever needed a doctor until a diphtheria epidemic struck us. It took several of the children in the neighborhood, among them little brother Ernest, five years old. We all had it but the rest of us recovered and were as good as ever when we got over it. When I was eleven years old and little Ernest was two weeks old we all took the whooping cough. Little brother was two weeks old and he was a very sick little baby for several weeks. Our mother would carry him on a pillow and had to watch him very closely when he had a coughing spell. There was danger of him choking to death. He was too weak to raise the phlegm in his throat. It seemed like when one of us began to cough it set the rest going. Then there was plenty of noise for awhile.

Later there was a case of smallpox in the neighborhood, so the children were to be vaccinated. I do not think it was compulsory but people would get frightened and take all the precaution they could. So when we heard the doctor was coming to vaccinate us, my younger brother and I, when we saw the doctor driving up the lane in his buggy, we hid in the tall rye where they could not find us. We watched when he drove away, then came back home. I do not remember if we were punished for it. If we were it was not severe enough to make an impression on us. So I never was vaccinated until after I was married. It made me very sick at that time and I was sorry that I did not have it done when I was a child. My father had the smallpox when he was a young man but it left no scars on his face like some cases we knew did.

Every one feared smallpox in those days. When the farmers had to market their crop by hauling them to the nearest market, which was the nearest city of a good size, some of them would sew small bags of sulfur in the waistband of their trousers, thinking that would prevent them from getting a contagious disease. It was not very pleasant to be anywhere near them when the weather was warm. How we hated the smell of sulfur. We were glad that our father did not have to do that. We felt pretty safe knowing that our father could take care of us if we should get it. No one would go near a home where they knew there was smallpox. So it was hard to get help, especially in the country. How good it is to know that horrible disease is almost stamped out at most places. We scarcely hear of a case these times. And it is indeed a blessing to know that it is handled so efficiently.

None of [us] children had the measles or mumps while we were children. Most of us waited until we had children of our own and had them when we were least able to take care of ourselves or our children. I had them when I had four little children of my own and I was very sick. The strangest thing about that was that we all had them within a year of each other although we were miles apart. After that we all thought it much better for children to have measles while they were young and able to outgrow bad results that measles sometimes leaves one.

My mother always provided [all] the home remedies for such as colds and coughs and stomach trouble that children have occasionally, especially at green apple time. We would gather elderberry blossoms when they were at their best and tie them in bunches and dry them in the loft. Mother would make tea of it and give it to us to drink. I do not know what medicinal purpose it had but it did seem to soothe a bad cough so we could sleep. Another remedy was horehound. That was harder to take, being so bitter. So we would take some of our sorghum molasses and make candy. My mother was troubled sometimes and she thought it helped her. We did not need to pick that and dry it. It was a hardy perennial and if one knew just where it grew we could find it in sheltered places all winter. That seemed to be my job. Mother would tell me to go and get some. I knew just where it grew. It grew along a fence among the tall grass where it was sheltered. I would scrape the snow away and the dry grass and I could find some nice young shoots or still some of the green stalks or leaves. I would make a strong tea of it and put a lot of molasses and some sugar and plenty of butter and make taffy or brittle candy. The little children did not like its bitterness.

Mother also kept remedies on hand for chapped hands and lips. She would save some of the mutton tallow when we killed a lamb for fresh meat. She would mix the tallow with gum camphor and melt it together and mold it in small cakes to use as we needed it. Then of course there was the goose grease for little children's chests when they were not old enough to object to being greased. How we did hate the smells of all these things.

Sister Lizzie, two years younger than myself, would have a spell of something we called phthisic, as we called it at that time. So she had to be careful about taking cold. Mother always dreaded to see her have a spell. There was danger of her choking. She would have it very bad at times. Until we all had the whooping cough my mother dreaded seeing her getting [ill]. She knew how hard it would be on her. But she was told that if Lizzie survived the whooping cough that she would not have it anymore. She was sick for a long time that summer but she never had the phthisic again. And we were all so glad that was over. She was not as strong and healthy as I was, so she had to be more careful about taking care of herself. But she grew up to be a healthy woman.

Brother Gus, two years younger than Lizzie, would have the

croup. When he had a spell of it we would all be very much frightened. He was healthy otherwise and grew up to be the tallest of all of us. He was also a good worker. Nothing ever was too hard for him to do. He never shirked his part of his work and was always on the job. His schooling was not all that he wanted. He and the young man teacher in the district became friends. Gus went to school to him. The teacher took an interest in him so Gus studied diligently and got through the grades and ready to go to Delaware College. He taught school between times during his college years and also after that for many years, and later he helped organize a bank and worked at that until he lost his health. He was married and lost both his boys after they had grown to young manhood. That grieved him greatly. He was sick a long time before he passed away.

When I was seventeen, Father decided to make a change, so we moved to a farm in the next county. It was a very productive farm. The land was good, so we were able to raise fine crops. The land was situated in the bottom along the East Fork of the Little Miami River. Our house stood on a bank close to the river but safe from any danger of being flooded. Mother never got used to the change and never felt right. She got sick with chills and fever or ague, as they called the disease. She thought it was caused by being too near the water and not being used to such a rough country. She imagined all kinds of dangers. There were high hills all around us and some very high and stony banks along the creek.

We youngsters were thrilled with all the surroundings and imagined or felt like we had moved to a different country. We liked the fishing and wading and swimming, for those that could. I never learned to swim but I did love to wade in the water in the summertime. Our brothers would sit on the bank near where we and the neighbor girls wanted to paddle around in a pond, [which was] about three or four feet deep with a sand bottom. We would get dressed for it and go after dark. And Tony would be near to see that nothing happened to us.

A little ways down the hill there was a grist- and sawmill. They ground wheat and corn and sawed lumber from logs hauled to them. The miller had two daughters about our own age, so we had a good time together. When no one but the miller was there we would get out on the carrier that carried the log for the saw to saw through until it went out over the race, [which is] the water that runs the mill. It was a daring thing to do. We realized it, but as long as we had the miller to watch that we did not get hurt. We would love to see him grind the wheat and corn. When we wanted cornmeal we would go to the crib and select the finest white ears of corn and shell a few grains of each end and then shell about a bushel or as many ears as would make that much. And that was a job—our hands would be pretty sore before we got through. But we had some fine, fresh meal for our cornbread and mush and corn cakes.

Father would take about five bushels of wheat to be ground for flour. That much would make a barrel of flour. I think it was that much after the miller took out his toll for grinding it. That left the miller with flour to sell where some had no wheat to grind. There were several such mills within a few miles. They are fast disappearing. It is too slow for these times and there are better ways of doing [it]. But are we better off or happier?

Chapter II

Farm Chores

End of winter

OUR WORK BEGAN IN THE LATE WINTER OR EARLY SPRING when the days were longer and the hens began to lay. I remember when it was freezing cold how we watched the hens so we could get the eggs before they froze. Sometimes we were not in time or could not find the nest in time. We would come in with a lot of frozen, cracked eggs. My mother would put them in cold water to thaw and she would fry them for supper with plenty of ham or smoked sausage. It seems to me that eggs never tasted better.

Gathering the eggs was sometimes a difficult thing to do. The hens would steal away and lay a nest full of eggs. Sometimes several hens would lay their eggs in the same nest. So there would be quite a lot of them. And when one of the hens got ready to sit on the eggs she would fight off the rest of them and begin to hatch her eggs that took twenty one days before they would hatch. And if this happened late in fall, we did not want the little chickens around when the cold weather came around [as] we had no brooder to keep them warm.

One time I discovered a nest of eggs under the stable floor which was at one end of the barn. I crawled under the barn and had enough room but the stable floor was a very tight squeeze to get under and I had to crawl over a large cross beam. I got to the eggs but to get back was not so easy. I had to go backwards and I could hardly get over that cross beam. I was getting frightened, but I knew there was no one around that would hear me if I did scream. So I wiggled out, a very mussed up and frightened little girl. After that I did not try such a thing again. After that when I found a nest of eggs where it was too hard to get at them I would take a rake or something that I could rake them out with, even if some were broken. I always got them, if it was possible. The stable floor boards were too heavy and well nailed down to try to take up a board to get at a hen's nest of eggs.

We were always glad when the days were longer so we could eat supper before we had to light the candles. We made our own candles. We had several molds. Some held two dozen, others one, and some three candles. We would save the tallow from the beef we had butchered earlier, then make the candles as we needed them. We children would help my mother string the molds, as we called it. It was by twisting a wick and doubling it loosely and putting it in the mold and pulling it out the other end through a small hole and tying it and then putting a straight stick through the loops at the top, and pulling it tight and sure so it would be straight and in the middle so the candle would be all right. My mother would fill the molds after they were strung with hot melted tallow so [those were] our lights for some years. I remember we children wanted to be on hand when the candles were to be pulled out of the molds. My mother would cut the knot at the small end and let us pull them out. We were very proud when they all came out perfect. But oh how those candles would drip and mess up our candlesticks. We had brass candlesticks, and they had to be clean and shining. I did not like the job of helping do that.

But it was not any worse than filling lamps with kerosene and keeping the lamp chimneys clean. Well I remember when my father brought home the first coal oil lamp. We were all afraid of it. My mother was very careful to put it up on the high mantel so none of us could reach it if we wanted to. Of course it gave us a better light to read by. But we still had candles and firelight in the big fireplaces. We had two such fireplaces. But we kept one going all winter and the one in the parlor only at times. It was a lot of work for the men folks to keep those huge fireplaces going. I often wonder how my father was able to bring in such huge logs for a back log. We always liked a good back log. It threw out more heat and kept a fire longer.

We would sit around the fire and our father would tell us stories. Some as I remember were hair-raising. But the more so the better. We liked them and begged for more. He would sing with us and taught us how to dance, and we had games such as checkers, dominoes, nine mill, and cards. Sometimes when my father wanted to read we would get too noisy and disagree over the game. Then they were taken away from us for awhile. Our father was not cross with us, and punished us seldom. When we did something that we knew deserved punishment we would run out and hide until we thought he had forgotten it. Sometimes he had not completely forgotten and thought it his duty to punish us. He would give us a glancing lick that did not hurt enough to cry over, then all was well again. We had many happy times together as children.

Spring chores

Our work began around the last of February or March the first. We would begin by soap-making. We would save the ashes we collected from our wood burning, then we would set up two barrels with holes bored in the bottom on a sloping platform so the lye could run in a trough or vessels for that purpose. First we would put a layer of straw a few inches thick in the bottom to serve as a strainer, then pack the ashes a layer at a time and then tamp them down firmly until the barrel was almost full. We left room at the top to pour water so it ran through the ashes after the ashes stood for a day or so to be well soaked. We would keep pouring water on them slowly as long as the ashes showed enough strength to hold up an egg. After we had enough lye collected we would pour it in a large iron kettle and boil it a while. Then it was ready for the fat. We would put enough fat in the lye when it would dissolve, no more, that was enough. Then after boiling awhile it would begin to thicken, then it was done. We would make a barrel of it enough to use for some time. That was what we called soft soap.

Later we bought the prepared lye that came in cans and made hard soap with it. That was less work and more satisfactory all around. My mother was careful about what kind of soap for our toilet. She liked castile soap best. We liked its smell. It seemed clean and pure. My mother thought when we had a wound or sore that washing it with castile soap was good for it. And it seemed to heal a wound.

Then there was getting ready to sit the hens on eggs to hatch around the first of April when we could expect sunshiny days for the little chicks. How they would enjoy the sunshine! At that time we would gather as much as six or seven dozen eggs a day. My mother would select the best looking of them to set so we could expect good strong chicks when they hatched. The hen would sit on them three weeks before they came out of the egg. In those days we had no incubators or brooders, so the hen had to do it all herself by we giving them a good coop for shelter and feeding. Of course we had to look after them to see that they were not caught out in hard shower or rain. The chicks could not stand getting wet before they [had] feathers enough to keep their skins dry. The hen had a hard time to keep them all covered after they had grown some.

Our poultry consisted of chickens, geese, ducks, and later turkeys and guineas. We raised the geese for their feathers. Picking the feathers every six weeks in the summer time was a task we did not enjoy. We would lie the goose on our lap on her back and by holding the feet and wings firmly with the head under our arm the picking would be done by picking the feathers from the breast and a few on the middle of the back. We had to be careful not to tear the flesh by pulling the feathers when they were ready to shed them. They were nice clean feathers for our pillows and featherbeds that were used in those days. We also picked the ducks but we kept their feathers separate. They were coarser and not so good for pillows.

The guineas were not so profitable, although a young one was good eating but oh, how tough if you tried to cook one a year or more old. Their eggs were good to eat if we could find them. They would steal their nests away in a field or a weed patch. We would follow them sometimes and find the nest. But we had to be careful so they did not see us.

The turkeys were hard to rear, so we did not bother much with them. We would have a young goose for our Christmas dinner and we enjoyed it. But they were so hard to dress and get ready for the oven and they did not lay many eggs. Anyway, we did not like the eggs to eat so they were kept mostly for their feathers. My mother gave [us] girls our pillows and featherbeds when we went to our own homes so we were sure of good clean beds. They lasted many years by having them cleaned and renovated at times.

At Easter time we would have baskets full of colored eggs. Each of [us] children when we were small would make our nests in the grass when the spring was early at Easter time and our eggs would be put in them. We would have our baskets ready, and what a scramble it was on Easter morning. My mother would save the onion shell for coloring. They made pretty different shades of brown, and our mother thought them safe for the little children to play with. She also used sassafras. They were a lighter shade and safe, too. We would dig the roots in the early spring and make tea. But we soon got tired of it. We would drink it for our health. Some thought in those days that it was good for the blood in the spring time after being shut up so long.

My mother wanted the best of the eggs that were laid on Good Friday to set. She said that they hatched out pretty chickens. But we knew that it was the right time to start raising chickens and the eggs were at their best at that time. Of course we had young chickens hatching out most all summer and early fall in order to have them for our use to fry or roast and some to sell on the farm. We usually sold enough butter and eggs and poultry to buy our groceries. That seemed to be the job or part of it for the farmers' womenfolk.

Next on the program was cleaning up the yard and garden and cellar, and getting the soil ready to plant a garden and make flower beds. We liked our flowers and always found time to plant as many as we could. They were part of our garden. We always had a long row along the center of the garden which divided the smaller early vegetables such as lettuce, radishes, onions, peas, bunch beans, carrots, beets, and summer turnips, a small patch of early potatoes and later pole beans, and late turnips, cabbage and a few other late vegetables. Such was our kitchen garden near the house where it was convenient for us to gather them for cooking. We were always glad for the first green things in the garden after a long winter of doing without them. My mother would say that we were like the cattle in that respect. They were always glad to get the first green grass in the early spring.

Then there was getting in the corn and potatoes, and everyone that was able to work [was] very busy. We were always careful in getting the best seed we could get. When we had a good variety of some vegetable we would save the seed [from] that certain plant. Lettuce seed was hard to save. The little yellow birds loved it and went for it even before it was ripe enough to gather. My mother would tie a thin cloth over it in order to save the seed.

We raised our onion sets either by planting seed or the tops of the old onions we had left from our winter's supply. We liked that way best. The seedlings were too tedious to raise and needed more care, such as keeping the weeds out and gathering them. It was much easier to just break the tops off than to get down and gather those small onions [like] the kind we buy these days. How we did hate to weed onions! When we did something that we thought needed punishment we would go out and weed onions when they were in season and how we did work. Of course it was work for youngsters. They could get at the rows better than a grown person.

I remember one time I was sent to a neighbor to get a jug of vinegar and I was careless in setting it down and it rolled down the hill and smashed on a rock. Of course I had to go home without the vinegar. I do not remember being scolded for it but I felt guilty anyway and how I did weed onions that evening. The task did not seem nearly as hard as thinking of my carelessness in losing that jug and vinegar.

After the seeds were planted and everything cleaned up outside came the house cleaning. Around the first of May that was a job that was hard on us. There was a lot of white-washing to do and the men folks being so busy they could not take time to help us, so we womenfolk tackled it ourselves instead of waiting for someone to help us. This was all extra work we had to do besides our daily tasks such as milking the cows and taking care of the milk and churning the cream in a dasher churn, which was good exercise when it was done right. Our mother taught us how to do it with steady, not too hard strokes. When the butter came easy, that was when the cows got plenty of good grass to eat. It was a pleasure to see the rich golden butter come out of the milk. To make good butter the cream had to be just right. That was harder to do in the winter time when it was harder to keep it at the right temperature.

Our mother was an expert butter maker and always got a good price for her butter. The store where we sold it knew Mother's print, and he wanted all he could get of it. Mother did not have butter molds like some. She preferred to work her butter until all the milk was worked out instead of washing it. It kept much longer that way. Most people washed their butter so that made my mother's butter different from washed butter. She would make her own print from a potato. She would cut it like a leaf of a tree and it was very pretty. I do not think anyone else copied it but we girls did in later years when we made our own butter. I know I used it when I had butter to make which is many, many years ago. But I still remember the fine butter I would take to the store where we bought our groceries. I remember how displeased the storekeeper was when we did not have the usual amount. He had his regular customers for it so it upset him when he could not supply them. He had been a Civil War soldier and had lost a leg. But that did not improve his temper or keep him from using his crutch for other than walking. He was well able to take care of himself in spite of the loss of one leg. But we got along very well with him as long as we brought him our butter and eggs and poultry that we had to sell.

I would drive once a week to the village. Sometimes when the other horses were all in use I would have to drive poor old blind Mollie. A blind horse is not much fun to drive. One has to be on the watch all the time so it will not get off the road. Our road through the wood was narrow and rough and if we did not watch we were apt to go over the bank. In that way a horse and wagon can be almost as dangerous as an automobile. In those days there were few good roads outside of the main pikes which even then were somewhat stony at places. But the worst horse to drive was a mare with a colt following, which we did sometimes. The mare was constantly looking to see if her colt was following all right. If we left the colt at home it would make such a fuss about it that the mother would seem to hear it and was uneasy constantly. I liked hitching up a good driving horse to a light wagon or buggy and going as I pleased and not have to hurry.

The next work we did after planting the spring crops was harvesting wheat, barley and rye, and later oats and hay. Every day brought its work and there was little time for anything but work for all that was able to work. There was the corn and potatoes to cultivate after the harvest and threshing was over. There was still some cultivating to do and get the soil ready for fall planting. And about the first of October there was corn cutting and potato digging and a little later corn husking. It was nice to see the cribs filled with fine yellow corn to feed the stock for the winter. With the mows filled with hay and plenty of fodder stacked around we were sure that the stock would have plenty to eat when winter came.

But to get back to potatoes, how we children did hate to plant potatoes or pick them up when they were being dug. Someone would plow them out of the ground. Then they would have to be gathered up and sorted, the largest ones for our table use, the next size for seed and the small ones to be boiled in a large kettle out of doors for the pigs. On a farm little need go to waste if it is managed right. Everything that grows has its use. We also fed some of the cooked potatoes to the chickens. Geese and ducks do not eat such food. Geese eat only grass and grain, mostly corn. They are usually fattened by stuffing them with corn and keeping them in a close pen.

Growing crops

When we were small children we would go out after dark on a hot, sultry night in July and sit on the top rail of the fence that surrounded the cornfield and listen to the corn grow. It would make a crackling sound as the blades unfolded. Mother would ask us what made us stay out so late. She knew that we needed all the rest and sleep we could get. Brother Tony would say that we were listening to the corn grow. I can still remember the sensation it gave us when we heard the sound of the corn growing. Corn grew best on the hot, sultry July nights especially when there had been plenty of rain. Crops do so depend on the weather.

In later years I owned a beautiful palm. It got too large for our bay window so I sold it and bought a small one which got very large, too. I always was interested in palms. When a new frond was showing I would watch it closely as it unfolded. As I was going about my work I would hear again the crackling sound of the corn growing and all at once it would unfold in a beautiful green fan. A growing plant is very interesting and shows the power of nature and of a higher power than we are.

We can plant and till the soil but we cannot make it grow. Nature is a higher power which we cannot give it. When we plant a little brown bulb or a little seed and see what springs from the soil it is indeed wonderful and it makes us think of the power of a higher being that gives us so many blessings on this earth. Everything that we need on this earth is given us if we strive earnestly to use these blessings as God meant them to make us happy. I often think of the many beautiful things we have on this earth and what a beautiful world this is, and to think how all these blessings are being abused by a few wicked men that seem to tear it up.

Getting wheat ready to be ground at the mill would be by running it through what we called a windmill, run by turning a crank by hand, which was very hard work. When we children were old and strong enough to do that, we would take turns in doing it. I do not know why the little grist water mills did not do that. I am sure there is a better way of doing it. There were no steam threshers around at that time so the grain was threshed by horse power. That is many years ago. This was done by hitching eight horses at a platform on a large cog wheel with four long poles extending from it. They would hitch two horses at each pole and a man would stand on the platform with a long whip-lash to touch up a horse that was inclined to lag and so was not doing his share in making the machine go that runs the thresher. They would have to stop to rest the horses so often. That made it slow going.

If a farmer had a big crop of grain, it made it several days of threshing. We would have to do the cooking for the men, which took a lot of work to feed so many. And the men that owned the thresher would stay for the night and that meant breakfast, too, and feed for the horses. The farmer would provide for a team or two to run the machine. After we moved to Clermont County there were still a few of the old treadmill horse power machines run by one horse, which I think was cruel to a horse that did very well where a farmer had a small job of threshing. I never saw any of those kind in Butler County where we had lived, where the land was better and larger crops were raised.

I think that was partly why Mother did not like Clermont County. It seemed too primitive to her. She had not been used to seeing so wild a country. There was more poor land and higher and stonier hills. But the farm we lived on was a good farm and we raised good crops, better than where we had lived. Mother's old friends and neighbors teased her and told her that she would starve and that the land would not raise beans. But that was not the case this time. The farms in the bottoms in Clermont County are as good as any bottom land anywhere else.

After the barley was threshed it would have to be bearded. That would be done by sweeping the barn floor clean and see that the cracks in the floor were taken care of. Then they would spread many bushels, I do not know how many. Anyway, it was a huge pile with a space bare in the center for a man to stand in to guide the two horses that would go around and around with the man in the middle turning the grain with a scoop shovel so as to keep it stirred up so it would all get trampled on to get the beards off. Then it would be run through the windmill to get it ready for market.

One can see how much better a way farmers have of doing their work these days. I do not know how it is done now. I have not been on a farm for fifty-five years. I am sure they have a better way of doing their work these times. In later years the threshing could be done in a shorter time when the steam engine came in use. Now where they have large crops of grain they have machines that thresh it as it is cut in the field. Think how much work that saves. I saw such a machine last summer as we were driving through the country and I thought what a different way of farming than we had when I lived in the country. I do not think the farmers have to work nearly as hard to raise their crops these days with all their modern equipment. But still there are still many things that machines cannot do. But machines are not so much work as horses were to take care of. When I see a poor horse hauled around in a truck I feel sorry for them. They look so humiliated.

We also raised rye. When Father wanted the straw to tie up bundles of corn fodder he would thresh some of it with a flail on the barn floor so it was left nice and straight. He would tie it up in bundles and keep it until he needed it. He would also get a good price for the rye straw at the paper mill and Mother liked the nice white straw for our beds. It was finer and would last longer and not lump up so badly. It always seemed to have less dust. Father would take some of the grain to the mill and have flour made of it. Mother could bake good rye bread by using part wheat flour with it. But I was always glad when we were out of rye flour. I liked the white bread better. But the rye bread was better for us. There is more nourishment in rye bread.

In those days harvesting grain was a lot of hard work. We did not have the implements to do the work like now, so when the farmer had a good bit of grain to harvest, he had to hire a lot of men to get it done in time when it was ready to harvest. We usually had three or more men to do what they called cradling. That was cutting it with an implement called a cradle. It was made with a sharp, long blade about three or more feet long and four or five wooden what they called teeth, the same length as the blade that was attached to a handle or snath, they called it. It was like a scythe. That way they could cut the grain without tangling it so it would lie straight in rows. A man would come behind each cradle with a rake, and rake enough to make a sheaf and tie it up. After that another man would come along and shock the grain. One man could take care of several cradles and binders.

Here was where the younger children could help by carrying sheaves on a pile of twelve sheaves. That made a shock, which was done by setting up ten sheaves with the heads up and cap[ping] that, [then] spreading out two sheaves on top of the rest firmly so the grain was protected from the rain until it was ready to be threshed or hauled in the barn or stacked in a big stack if they could not get it threshed. Soon enough that was done to keep it from spoiling in the field. How times have changed, and for the better. Now the grain can be cut and threshed all at one time, saving a lot of work for everyone. I remember the first reaper my father had. We thought it [was] wonderful. But soon it was still better by having a binder attached. So there was only the shocking to do. We never had a thresher.

Harvest time was a busy time even for the children on a farm. There was water to carry to the men every hour or so. It usually was very warm and they worked hard, so [they] got very thirsty. They would start at daybreak, which was very early at that time of the year. So they would get hungry at about ten o'clock, so there was a lunch to fix for them. So that was a child's job, too. The lunch was light, just some bread and cheese or cold meat with a fresh drink of water or buttermilk for those that would drink it. My father did not like buttermilk, so he drank water with his lunch. Their days were long. They worked from sunup until sundown, with one hour rest at noon and another half hour out for supper at five o'clock, and then out to work again sometimes as long as they could see. There was no such thing as eight or ten or even twelve hours. The women's work was as hard. Sometimes a lot of that had to be done by candlelight.

This brings us up again to the fall. Our father would plant a patch of sorghum, and when it was ready to be cut and stripped of the blades there was work for the children again. We would strip the blades from the stalks, then father would cut it down and cut the heads off and tie it up in bundles so it could be loaded on the wagon and hauled to the mill where they made the molasses. We had enough for two barrels of molasses, one for us and one for the people that made it. That made plenty for us and some to give away to neighbors that did not bother with making it. When my father went for the molasses we children would go with him. The people that made it would give us a small wooden paddle that they kept for that purpose so we could eat the taffy around the outside of the pans. We did not care much about it that way. We much preferred to make our own taffy later on. When the weather was cold we would parch a big pan of corn and then cook the molasses and put it on the corn so each of us had a huge ball of it. It was very good. I often wonder if our children now days would enjoy it as much as we did. We were too far from any place where we could buy candy so we had to make it when we wanted some. But I remember how good the sticks of mixed candy [were] that our father would bring us when he went somewhere where he could buy it. It was a change from the homemade stuff we made.

In those days we thought cakes and bread that came from a bakery were a great treat even if we had better at home. My father would plant a patch of buckwheat for our bees. We had a few hives of them for several years. But my father decided that they were too much bother for an amateur to take care of. The blossoms of the buckwheat [were] for the bees to gather their honey from. We liked that brand of honey. We also liked clover honey. But we did not like the honey from locust trees. The buckwheat seed would be taken to the mill to be ground for our winter's supply of buckwheat cakes, and it was very good. We were fond of them with sausage on cold winter mornings. Mother would make the batter the night before with yeast. They were very light and tender. Our sorghum came in good to eat with them. When we thought the bees had run out of honey, their natural food, we would feed them buckwheat flour and sugar to keep them from starving.

When folks would get ready to take the honey from the hive early in the summer, so the bees would still have time to gather their own winter's supply, we would keep at a distance. The bees being disturbed were not any too safe for us being too near them. My brother Tony was allergic to any kind of bee sting. It would make him sick when he was stung by them. And still he would not keep away from a bumble [bee] nest. Sometimes his face would not look like a human face when he was stung by them. His eyes would be swollen shut and his whole face out of shape. The bumble bees were troublesome in a hay field or along a rail fence or a stone wall. He would not quit until he had routed them all out. He hated them for what they did to him. So he destroyed them whenever he could. He and any kind of bee did not get along together. I was not much afraid of them. They did not seem to bother me much, although I was stung several times, but not bad enough to care much or be afraid of them. But at the same time I did not bother them either.

I was more afraid of snakes, and we all hated them and killed them whenever we could, which we found out later was a mistake. Large black snakes they say are the farmer's friend. They destroy rats and mice and other varmints. But we did not like the crawly things. Father did not hate them and did not kill them. There was a big black snake that was in a potato patch. Father would see it every time he went there and the snake did crawl away when it saw him. It had gotten used to seeing him there, but one day Sister Clara went there to get some potatoes. She saw the snake and promptly killed it. Father was sorry and said "Oh, did you kill my snake?" But he laughed about it. He had not told us it was there.

One day I went to get some potatoes from a patch close to the woods. I heard a rustling in the leaves over the fence. I looked and saw a snake swallowing a toad, and was having an awful time getting it down. I knew that snakes did eat toads and I liked the toad better than I did the snake, so I took the hoe and chopped the snake's head off and again as near as I knew the toad was, so the poor toad could get out if it was still alive. It was alive and hopped away. I realize that this sounds fantastic, but it is the truth. So many unbelievable things can happen in the country. I could tell many more that I know you would not believe.

My mother's health began to fail, and it often fell to me to look after much of the farm work. Sister Lizzie could help, too. Then the younger girls could do their part, too. There was a job for everyone that was able to work. So we got along very well and were a happy family together. This takes me back a few years again. When Sister Lizzie and I were old enough, Father would take us with him when he hauled a load of grain to market in the city. Sometimes it was one, and again both of us. I have wondered why he wanted to bother but he seemed to want us with him. He said that we could watch the horses and the load while he was bargaining with the market people. When he hauled the barley to the brewery the sale was bargained for beforehand, so that was easier. He would take us around and show us what barley was used for but it did not make us like beer. We hated the bitter stuff.

When he took the wheat to the flour mill, that was more interesting. Potatoes were taken to the market and sold to grocery keepers and whoever would buy them, so that took a little longer to get rid of the load. When we went to town we would have to get up long before daylight and [it might] be sometimes very late at night before we got home again. I remember when I was about eight years old I went to the city with father and it turned quite cold and it rained and turned to sleet. We had no covered wagon. Father piled the bags in the corner of the wagon near the front where he could keep near me. I was bundled up pretty well, and had a waterproof cape on that covered me pretty well, and kept me dry. I kept very quiet. I remember father calling to me quite often to see if I was all right. We got home late but safe, and when we were warmed up and slept the rest of the night no bad effects were felt.

It was just as hard to drive a team that did not have sharp shoes on an icy road as it is an automobile now days. I remember when they wanted to take the horses out in the winter time they would have to be rough shod. They would not take them out on the road if they were not. Sometimes it would be only the front shoes, but if they were going any distance it would have to be all around. The blacksmith would be very busy in the winter time when the roads were slick. Sometimes a horse would lose a shoe and it would have to be taken to the smith to be put on so the horse would not break his hoof and be lame. A horse cannot walk on a stony road without shoes very long. It would be cruel to make them do it.

Many years ago when I was a small child, a well-to-do farmer in the community built a slaughterhouse, and the farms for miles around sold their hogs to him when they were ready for market. They were butchered and taken to the packers dressed and ready for whatever they wanted to do with them. His help came from the farmers and other men in the community he could get. The farmers were glad to earn some cash in the winter time when they were not so busy with crops. They would also haul the dressed hogs to town so that needed some good sharp horseshoeing when the roads were icy. At that time the meat did not have to be inspected so carefully as now so they were able to kill and dress the hogs at home which cannot be done [now]. And it seems to be a good thing.

One year or several years an epidemic of hog cholera swept through the country and took many hogs, which was a great loss to the farmer. One year father had his bunch of hogs fattened and almost ready for market. The cholera came and took them all, even the ones for our own meat for most of the year. Father had fed most of the corn he had for that purpose, so that was gone, too. The chickens took it, too, and so there were not enough of them left for our own use. The disease took the chickens quite often, so we were never sure that we would get to keep them. We fed them with everything that we heard was good for them, but sometimes it did not help. I know how worried we were when we saw the buzzards flying around when the disease was anyways near us. We were sure that they carried it to other farms. We would get so sick of seeing dead hogs and chickens around and it was a problem how to get rid of them. They would take them as far as they could to some ravine and bury them the best they could. Whenever they could, they would burn them. It took a lot of wood and time.

It seemed like the farmer was doomed sometimes. But perhaps the next year was much better, so they would begin all over again. The farmer had to be brave. He did not get help from the government like now. The farmers these days are different than they were some seventy-five or a hundred years ago. Everything depended on his own hard labor. He did not have the tools and other conveniences he has now. And the crops were much harder to tend and to market. I remember when the large platform spring wagon came in use. It was larger and easier to ride on and they could haul bigger loads than they could on the jolt wagon. But think what an advantage the motor truck is over that now. So I think it is much easier to farm these days. The farmer now has most all the advantages of the city man and gets to live in the country, too. But still the city man goes to live in the country and some country people come to the city where they think they can do better. So it is very well that we do not all want the same thing. Easy transportation makes it easy to live wherever we please.

It was not easy to farm successfully at any time for a man that rented a farm. He had to have his rent money ready, regardless of failure of crops. The land owner would have a mortgage on his stock and farming implements for security, and when he put the note in the bank the money had to be forthcoming within thirty days. They seemed to be strict about that. Sometimes the farmer could not keep his crops for better prices, so there was a loss there. Sometimes the rent would come due twice a year, the first of September and the first of March. The grain crop had to be sold before the first of September to meet that payment and the fat hogs for the first of March. Sometimes they would farm for shares. But that was a bother, too. So all in all it was not easy either way. But if we could leave all the unpleasant things out we would not be able to appreciate the better things. And after all I think a farm is a good place to bring up a large family.

One year the corn crop failed at many places, ours among them. Father had a bunch of hogs that had to be fattened, and we had plenty of potatoes that year. He would cook large kettles of potatoes and wheat and barley and oats. He had two large iron kettles down under the willow tree some distance from the house. He fed them that, so he fattened them that way. It made them pot-gutted so their bellies would almost touch the ground when they walked. I do not know what kind of pork that made. Anyway, he got a good price for them, ten dollars a hundred. Pork was scarce that year. After father sold them he came home with a five hundred dollar bill. He showed it to me and let me handle it. It is still the largest bill I ever saw and the only one of anyways near that size. We were small children then and very curious, but some of us seemed to know the value of it.

Sugaring

One spring Tony and Gus decided that they wanted to make some maple syrup. So they assembled their equipment and started out. They had helped our uncle one year so they thought that they knew all about it. So they began tapping the trees and set their spills and the buckets ready to collect the sap from the trees. They had scalded and scoured what had been a pork barrel to put their sap in until they got ready to boil it down to syrup. They had hung two large iron kettles to boil it in. You see, they were not going about it in a big way. They just wanted to see if they could make a gallon or two. But it did not turn out so well especially when they had to stay with it all night so none of the sap would be lost. We girls thought we would go and help them. We stood it to about midnight. Then the woods seemed too dark and eerie for us, so we went home and left the boys to do it alone.

All would have gone pretty well if it had not been for the pork barrel. When their first batch of syrup was done, lo and behold, it was salty. So that was spoiled. But they did not give up and kept on. But they did not put any more sap in the barrel. After that they would boil it down until it was nearly done. Mother would finish it on the stove in the kitchen so we had some pretty good maple syrup after all. And with it all they had the opportunity to watch the small animals at night in the woods. They caught an opossum and did not know what to do with it. There was no colored man to get it so it went to waste. They had enough of trying to make maple syrup and never tried it again.

Cordwood

One year father cleared a piece of ground that had been a sugar camp. The trees were most all dead so there was a lot of nice wood. Father and a man that he hired chopped down the trees and sawed and split them up in cordwood, then hauled it down to the canal to be shipped to the city to the bakeries. In those days the bakers used nice clean, sound wood to do their baking. We children that were old enough would love to go and see the men chop the trees down and watch them fall, and then see how big a chip they could make.

There were some expert wood choppers in those days. Father was one. He could use his left hand as well as his right. So he could chop with a man that was right or left handed equally as well. When they cut down a green tree we would gather up the largest chips to be used in the smokehouse to smoke the meat, it being at the time when it was needed. We would watch father rick up the wood and measure it. There were many cords of fine wood, and father sold it for five dollars a cord, four feet by four by eight long. Now when we buy wood for our fireplaces they do not sell it that way. We get only half the amount for a cord unless we tell them about [it]. Then they say that they sell it by the rick.

Sometimes when there was snow on the ground they would haul the wood on a sled made low for that purpose. They would haul it on that for our use. We children would like to ride on the empty sled when we had the chance. One time I fell between the cross pieces of the sled and the sled passed over me without hurting me the least bit. But father was frightened and [saw] to it that it did not happen again. We were interested in the canal boats where father hauled his wood. We had friends that lived not far from the canal and when we visited them it gave us an opportunity to watch the boats creep along. We thought it a slow way to travel for even those days. The little mule would walk slowly along the towpath, guided by a man. It did not need much guiding. There seemed to be nothing else for him to do but follow the narrow path that many trips had worn down until it was quite deep at some places.

The people that ran the boat would live on it. We could see the women hanging washed clothes on the roof. The canal was not a very sanitary stream, and there seemed to be a lot of chills and fever or ague as they called it at that time. And I think it was a good thing to do away with it for more than one reason besides slow travel. In the winter time they would cut ice on it and fill large ice houses for summer consumption. [It] also seems [that] would have been injurious to good health. I often think and am glad that I have lived to see as many better ways of doing things to add to better health for our nation.

Sewing clothes and shoes

Sewing was a problem for Mother until we girls were old enough to learn to sew and be a help in making our own clothes. We learned quite young. We were taught by beginning to sew quilt patches. We would save up every scrap of calico or gingham and muslin we could get hold of. Sometimes we would exchange with neighbors so as to get all kinds of pieces to make a scrap quilt begun by piecing a nine-patch. That was the easiest pattern for a beginner. I had such a quilt pieced before I was nine years old. But I was not very proud of it, as I knew that I could do better than that. Later Mother wanted me to quilt it because it was the first sewing that I did. So after I had a home of my own I quilted it and wore it out. But I had other better ones by that time and wore them out, too. So now I have none of my old-time quilts to hand down to my girls. I am not interested enough to make any more, although I have plenty of time for doing it.

Well I remember when father bought us our first sewing machine. It was a low arm Singer. We were thrilled with it, but none of [us] girls were old enough to run it, so that was left for Mother to do. At first she had a hard time to sew a straight seam, and she thought it was a waste of thread and time when there was a lot of ripping to do. But we learned very young to run the machine. But Mother still kept us at hand sewing as much as she could. She was afraid that the machine would spoil all our inclination for hand sewing, and she did not want us to do that. Clara, being the oldest, learned first. I was next in line but I was four [years] younger and it was several years before I was old enough to run the machine.

There usually [was] a woman in the neighborhood that did sewing, so Mother would hire her to come and help out when we were in need of clothes and mother had no time to do it. Aunt Maggie was a dressmaker and she would help with our Sunday clothes, as we called our best clothes in those days. The girls in those days were supposed to begin wearing stays, in other words, corsets. I remember the first one that was bought for me. Aunt Maggie had insisted and thought mother was neglectful of me for not making [me] wear it. I hated them and would not wear one for every day. I felt imprisoned in one. I did not mind when I dressed for certain occasions. I was not a stout girl. That came when I was older.

We wore a lot of clothes those days and they all had to be made at home. We could not go to the city to buy them ready-made. There were full petticoats, two at least, besides the other pieces of underwear. The petticoats had ruffles and lace and tucks on the ruffles, all to be made ourselves. The problem of dressing us when we were growing up was even worse than when we were little. My mother was relieved when we were able to do our own sewing. She would say that she felt safe now that her girls could sew. We were glad to find the time to sew, especially when we were making a dress that we thought would look well on us.

Mother also made the boys' clothes. I remember how she would stay up to stitch a coat for Tony. She wanted it to look well, so she took great pains with it. She also made their jeans and cotton trousers. There were their shirts and underwear also all to be made. True, we did not have as many changes as is required now. It never could have been accomplished if we did. But we had enough, with a lot of laundering, which was another hard job with so many to keep clean. Then there were our shoes and stockings and gloves and hoods which we wore to keep us warm. Mother did not knit our stockings. She bought the most of them. And Grandma was a fine knitter. She would knit some when we were small children.

Shoes were another problem. The least we could have was two pairs, one substantive pair for every day that would stand the snow and mud in the winter time, and one better pair for Sundays or when we dressed up. There was an old soldier that was a shoemaker that had a shop in the village that made our everyday shoes while he was living. At that time the men wore high-top boots and the tops were pretty good after the bottoms were worn out, especially their dress boots. When Mother had them she would take them to the man and he would make us very good, everyday shoes to wear when we had to go through the mud and snow. Mother was careful to keep us well shod, as she would say. She did not want us to have wet shoes. This man would make them with high tops and leather laces with a good tongue to keep the snow out. They would have to be greased about once a week to keep them soft.

The boys wore boots most of the time as soon as they were old enough. And what proud little boys they were when they got their first pair of boots, especially if they had copper toes. They could kick as hard as they wished, and they had to kick sometimes when they pulled them after they had gotten them wet. They would get hard and shrink. They had a boot jack to pull them. It was no easy job to pull the boots off a sleepy little boy. He would come in cold, and when he got warm he would get sleepy before it was time to undress for bed. The men folks had a job keeping their boots soft by rubbing and greasing them until they were soft.

One pair of shoes that I have never forgotten was a fine soft kid side-lace that fit like a glove. They were size four, and I was very fond of them. We wore no low shoes then. Then we wore a shoe that was made from cloth that they called Purnell. Mother always wore them for a dress shoe. They were very dressy. They had high tops and were tedious to lace. In fact the shoes were all that way and when we were in a hurry to get dressed it was not so good. But such was the way we were shod. Mother most always had her shoes made. We had a very fine shoemaker in the village other than the soldier. Mother always had him make her shoes. They would fit and were very comfortable and they also wore well. But of course they were expensive, being custom-made and sewed by hand. But it paid her well by their comfort and long lasting quality.

Another problem for Mother was when we became at the age when it was time to put on our stays and our dresses lengthened. We girls did not get our growth at an early age, at least not as early as some girls did. When we were thirteen or fourteen our dresses were lengthened to halfway between the knee and ankle, then a year or two later to the shoe tops, and another year older to the ankles, then when full-grown to the floor. And with several girls coming on, it kept Mother busy. And what a nuisance those long dresses were. We did a lot of walking in those days. When we had a load to carry and hold up our skirts to keep them out of the mud, [it] was not easy. I think the styles now are much more sanitary and better all around. If only they had not gone to the other extreme quite so far.

This is something about our beds. We in the country did not have mattresses. We had what they called straw tick and a featherbed. Those kinds of beds were not easy to make up every morning. The straw had to be stirred up evenly and the featherbed fluffed up evenly. But our beds were comfortable and clean. Once a year or oftener our ticks were washed and filled with clean straw, usually right after threshing. Our beds would be fresh and high. We loved to get in the fresh beds when they were newly filled. When I was a small child we still had a trundle bed for the smallest children of the family. It would be pushed under Mother's bed during the day time and with a bed banion it would be put out of sight.

We children liked the trundle bed. It was easy to get in and it was near Mother's bed. We were like all young children and did not like to get far away from our mother, especially at night. Mother always kept us as near to her as she could. She most always had one baby in bed with her and the smaller not far away. But I do think the way they take care of babies now is better for their health.

Chapter III

Animals on the Farm

Horses

IN THOSE DAYS WHEN WOMEN WENT CALLING they rode horses and wore their long riding habits and used what they called side saddles made for that purpose. My mother could ride and was not afraid to attempt to ride a fiery horse as we called them. In those days the roads were not good enough to drive a wagon or buggy so a horse could get through better. There was a lot of horseback riding by the women as well as the men.

My father bought a black horse called Tom. My father bought him, not knowing his tricks. He would go pretty good for some time, and then all at once would stop, and all the coaxing or leading or even punishing him would not make him budge. He was [what] they called a balker. He did the same when they tried to ride him. He even kicked up his hind heels and if they did not watch and hold on the bit, they would go flying over his head. My mother rode him and he behaved all right. So they decided that he was used to have women ride him. Some horses objected to the women's long flapping skirts. But he did not seem to mind that. He was not used as a farm horse so my father soon got rid of him. There was a lot of horse trading in those days and they were not always good bargains when you bought sight unseen or untried. Few of them were what you wanted in a good horse. But there was not much money lost or gained in such a trade. It was always something that you wanted to get rid of at any cost.

Here is something [about] some of the really good horses we owned. One especially was Sallie. She was almost human and very dependable. My father always used her when he made the furrows to plant the corn. He could depend on her to help him make the furrows straight. He would place a stake with a white or red rag at the top of it at each end and in the middle if the rows were very long. When he got to one end of a row, he would measure about four feet and place the stake for the next row. Sallie would walk straight with her head to one side so my father could see the stake, and then walk straight to it and touch it with her nose. He had to speak very little to her or guide her. She knew just what to do, so that made it easy for my father to make a straight row.

In those days they made the furrows both ways so the corn could be tended both ways. It made it easier to keep the weeds out. We children helped plant the corn, so by having the cross furrows we knew just where to drop the corn. One day it was when they were building the Big Four railroad. It ran at one end of the farm we were living on. Father was making the furrows and I was dropping the corn behind him. They were blasting rock out of a deep cut that they had to make through a hill. We did not know that they were blasting at that time until we heard the noise and saw the rocks flying all around us. Sallie was very much frightened as well as we were. She ran with the plow, and my father hanging on, and me running as fast as I could so nothing happened that time. We were very careful after that that there was no blasting going on when they were working in that field. One of our favorite cows, Blackie, strayed too close and got killed. Of course we were very much grieved about it. We had raised her and she was a great pet.

We were very much attached to our animals especially when we had raised them ourselves. They were almost like one of the family. At one time my father had raised two fine iron gray mares and thought he would have a fine team when they got old enough to break to harness. But they did not turn out well. They were Julie and Dolly. My brother had made a pet of Julie. He would ride standing on her back and fold his arms. She would walk proudly and steadily, and seemed to enjoy it as much as he did. But Dolly was too mean for anything. She would not be broken to harness. As soon as they got the bit in her mouth and the harness on, she would begin to kick and rare until she had kicked herself completely out of the harness. And if she could not get them off she would lie down so no one could do anything with her. My mother would be so worried when they said they were going to hitch up Dolly again. She was so afraid that they would get hurt. She was vicious. My father sold her to a drover that bought horses and cattle, so we never heard anything more about her. And we were glad to part with her. Julie got sick and died, so there went the nice young team.

Later my father bought a white horse that was not so young. He was a very dependable horse but tricky at times. His name was Bob. At the same time we owned another bay horse, Prince. Bob did not like Prince and would fight him every chance he had. One day my brother and I were sitting on top of the rail fence under a tree. Bob was there so I got on his back and sat there talking to my brother. Suddenly Bob spied Prince at the other end of the pasture and made one leap for him. I flew over his back and sat on the ground. I was not hurt luckily. My brother said he believed that if I had been killed he could not have helped laughing the way I flew off his back. Poor Prince was so frightened that he ran for the barnyard and against the closed gate and broke it down and got tangled up in it. But [he] was safe in the barnyard.

Another horse I remember which we owned was Tom, a large white horse. He was gentle and a good horse to drive or work at the plow or any other place wherever he was hitched. Soon after my father bought him we discovered that he was afflicted with a weak heart. So we were constantly on the watch when we were driving him to ford the creek or along a steep bank, always afraid that he would drop and cause a very bad accident. So one day he did pass out suddenly, but not at a place where there was any danger.

Another large sorrel young horse that we had raised was the meanest one of all. He was not to be trusted anywhere. He even bit if you passed in front of his manger. He would reach over and grab me with his big teeth. One day Sister Lizzie and I were in the barn gathering the eggs, a job that we did every evening. He reached over as we were passing in front of him and grabbed sister by her head. Luckily she had a stiff sun bonnet on but she was injured and was sick for quite a while after the accident. One day I got on his back with only a halter to hold him. He started off with me holding on the best I could. But I finally slid off on his neck with my arms around his neck and hanging down in front of him. He bumped up against [the] gate. But I was not injured much. My father saw it and was very much frightened, and forbade me ever to get on his back again.

We made pets of our young colts which we brought up so when it became time to break them to harness they knew pretty much what was expected of them. As far as riding them, we did that as soon as they were strong enough to carry us. But it was an anxious time when we had a colt to break at the plow. My mother was constantly afraid that my father or the boys would get hurt. My oldest brother liked horses and was not afraid of them and could get them to do pretty much as he wished them to do.

My oldest brother, two years older than myself, was seldom sick and, like myself, [was] strong and healthy. We could do many things together so that made me somewhat of a tomboy, as a neighbor called me. This neighbor would say "hello, tommy," and I did not like that. He had a daughter about my age. He called her tom, too.

We both liked to ride horses. She could ride better than I could. In fact that was about all she did. She would get on her horse and ride all over the country. I only rode our horses around on the farm. When we were young children we would go to the field when it was time to quit for a meal or in the evening so we could ride on the horses. The men folks were good about it and did not mind bothering about us. Lizzie and I would both be helped on poor old Charlie and ride him. He had a tender spot on his back near his tail where the hair was rubbed off, so we had to be careful not to touch it or let our dress brush it. If we did, he would switch his tail and kick up. We were apt to fall off if he did. I think that the boys teased him and he was nervous. He was not a good horse to drive a light wagon so he was never used for any other purpose but pulling a heavy load and at the plow. He was what they called a good work horse.

Father owned a beautiful young bay mare that he had reared. She was nearly ready to be broken to harness when she was struck by lightning and killed. The storm frightened her and she came to the gate and tried to get near the horses in the stable but was driven away by our hired man. She ran back in the pasture and was killed. It seems we had bad luck with some of our best horses.

Another we had was a fine iron gray horse. A young horse also ready to break, she tried to jump over a paling fence and became impaled and was injured so badly that she had to be killed. Another one was a mare with a young colt. Father let her live long enough until the colt could be weaned. Her leg never mended and she died later. But it was terrible to see her suffer so much. And our good old Sallie ran a piece of splinter of wood just above her hoof that went down in her hoof and made her very lame. Father got a veterinarian and they threw her and fastened her down so as they could work on her foot but he could not get it out. So she was very lame. Father would poultice it and did everything he could to help her. She finally got better and was useful for a long time after that. Sometimes a poor horse would have a toothache and we could see that they suffered. They could not eat their corn. I do not remember what was done for that.

We could always tell when a horse had been in the Civil War. Many years after the war was over we would see a poor old horse trying to act young by prancing around whenever he heard a band playing. It made no difference where he was hitched, at a plow or cart or wagon. When he heard a brass band playing a march he would try to keep step with it. It was an odd sight to see a poor old horse trying to act like a colt. They were like the soldiers. They never forgot their war days. Some of the horses that the Morgan men left behind as they were going through had been fine horses, and when they were rested and doctored up became good horses again. They had been some that the raiders had stolen elsewhere on their raids.

A beautiful horse all spruced up in a parade is a beautiful sight. That was the thing I enjoyed most when we went to see a parade. They seem to know what is required of them and love to show what they can do. They also look for some reward when they have done something they were proud of themselves. We see so few nice horses now. The race horses are not the best looking horses. They have to be kept slim so they can go fast. The finest, well-kept horses I ever saw were the big draft horses they drove at the fire engines and the brewery and delivery trucks. They looked and were powerful animals and could draw huge loads. They also knew what was required of them and were well trained.

Cattle

There are more tales I could tell about the horses we owned, but [I] will stop here and tell something about other farm animals we owned, especially some of our cows. Cows and horses are the most essential animals on a farm. It would not be much of a farm without them. One of our favorite cows we owned was Blackie. She was a great pet with [us] children. One evening after dark, there came up a thunderstorm. The thundering and lightning was very sharp. Poor Blackie became frightened and sought to be with us. Someone had left the gate open, so she came to the kitchen window where she could see us in the room. She looked in and just then my sister Clara looked out in the dark stormy outdoors and saw a black face with large scared eyes. She gave a scream that frightened us all. But my mother saw what it was. But it took quite a while before our mother could convince us it was not a black ghost looking in on us from the storm out of doors.

Another favorite cow we owned was old Rony. She was a large roan cow and very sensitive. She was boss of the herd and would stand for no foolishness. She had to be first to be milked and was very particular who should milk her. She liked my mother best of all and did not like a man to milk her. She was all right as long as we did not try to pet her. When it was milking time and she saw us coming to do the milking, she would come to the gate and foot, that is, putting the right foot back of the left foot ready to milk always from the right side. If we stood and talked or did not pay attention to her she would sniff and be very out of patience and somewhat ill-tempered. She had her stall in the stable and the chain had to be laid so she could put her head through it so you could hook it up. If we did not do it quickly she would get angry and throw up her head. We had to watch out so she did not hit us with her horns. She had one crumpled horn. She was injured when she was young. We youngsters all respected old Rony. She was a good cow and gave us a lot of good milk.

We usually named our cows by their color. Rose would be a kind of yellowish color. Reddy, Spotty, Specky, Brindle, Cherry, Roany, Muley, a cow born without horns. Of course all cows are born without horns. But a real muley was one that never developed horns. In those days we did not de-horn cattle. They kept their horns so they could defend themselves very well, but sometimes became dangerous. In later years they began to de-horn them, a painful and I think cruel thing to do to a good self-respecting cow.

We owned one cow that no one would want to keep. There was always the drover that came around so when we had one that we did not want to keep she was sold to the cattle drover. So you see what a risk it was to buy from a drover. But they were usually sold to the slaughterhouse to go for beef. So they were prepared by extra feeding to get them in good condition for good meat. Sometimes we would lose a good cow by his eating too much green clover in the morning when the dew was on it or in the fall by breaking into a cornfield and eating too much green corn. They would become foundered, as we called it then. If we saw it in time they could be saved by stabbing them in the soft spot near the hip bone and the spine. Not all cows would founder. So when we had one like that, we would sell her. We did not feel like we could risk losing her, so she was sold to the drover or butcher.

A foundered cow

We owned several cows that had to be closely watched in the spring of the year when they would eat new grass early in the morning when the dew was still on it. They would eat it too fast and then their stomachs would become swollen and there was danger of losing them if we did not see it in time. When we saw it in time the cow could be stabbed on that soft spot near the spine, and the gas would come out and the cow was saved. We had a young cow that had been clovered, and Father saved her but before the wound had entirely healed the same thing happened again. None of the men folks were where we could call them so Sister Lizzie and I thought rather than let the cow die we would try to save her ourselves. So she went for the sharp butcher knife and she tried it but she could not. So I took the knife and stabbed her in the old wound and she was saved again. So we took care of the wound until it was healed nicely, and after keeping her awhile she was sold to the drover. She was a nice young animal and would make good beef. But anyway we were rid of her. We lost several cows that way.

A farmer had a lot of risk to run and is liable to lose a good cow or horse, which is a big loss. It takes two years to rear a cow before she can be of any use and it takes three years before a horse is old enough to be broken to harness, and then there is the risk of breaking them, as they are good horses for certain work we want them to do. They do not always turn out well. So that is a loss, too.

Meat

Meat was not inspected like it is now. And there were always a small butcher shop in the community where we could get fresh meat when we wanted it. That way we usually knew what kind of beef cattle they bought so the farmer could rear them to suit the purpose. Sometimes a farmer would prepare one for our own use and we would butcher a beef in the fall when the weather turned cool. Several of the neighbors would do the same thing but not at the same time, so we could exchange meat so it lasted a while. We could have it fresh for some time and we did enjoy a lot of steaks and roasts. Then we would prepare some for corned beef that would keep until the next summer. It was very good. My mother would get a large piece from the jar of brine and soak it and then cook it tender. It was good sliced cold and we enjoyed it the next spring or in harvest time.

Then there was the dried beef. We enjoyed that in the summer time when fresh meat was hard to keep. Then there was bologna. We had that when we could get a real butcher to make [it]. There was an old man, they called him Butcher John, so we had bologna when we could get him to make it. I can still remember the pepper he put in it. We would buy the whole pepper grains and grind it. It was very hot, so we children did not like it. A little went a long way. With the dried and pickled meat and the smoked hams and bacon and a keg of salt fish now and then and plenty of fresh eggs and chicken, we fared very well for meat in the summer time.

We also reared sheep and had a young lamb in the spring for some fresh meat when we wanted. I do not remember ever butchering a calf, but some farmers did. They are one animal I never cared much about, they were so messy to feed. Lambs were better. Although they could be very much of a nuisance when we raised them by hand. Sometimes when a sheep would have twins or triplets she would disown one or even two, and we hated to let them die. My father would give them to us to rear. They were cute but such a nuisance. They wanted to follow us everywhere, even in the house if we let them. We became attached to them and when it came time to sell them with the rest of the lot we were grieved to think that they would be killed.

Our winter meat was not a problem. Pork was the meat used. We would do our butchering as we called it at that time just before or during or shortly after the holidays. We always dreaded that job. It always meant a lot of messy and hard work. First there was the killing of the pigs and dressing them. The farmers at that time were the butchers. The neighbors would get together and exchange their services until all had their butchering done and exchange fresh meat with those that were waiting for some reason to do it later in the winter so the fresh meat lasted longer. After the pigs were dressed and cooled which would not be until the next day they were cut up in hams, shoulders and bacon, and salted firmly in barrels. That was the pork barrel to be smoked after six weeks in the salt. Then there was the lard to be cut up and rendered out and put in cans or jars to be kept until next butchering time. There was sausage to make, head cheese, mincemeat and several other things to be taken care of, the small meats or offals as some called them such as spare ribs, backbones and feet to be used first. We pickled the feet to be used later. We children did not like them. Then there were scraps that could not be eaten, so they were used to make soap later on but had to be cleaned and dried and packed in a keg for that purpose.

You can see what a greasy messy job butchering was. We were all glad when it was over so we could enjoy the fruits of our labor. We did enjoy having that good meat to use in cold weather. With the vegetables stored in the cellar we fared very well. Our cellars in those days were not so large as they should [have] been. There were bins for potatoes and other vegetables such as turnips and beets and carrots and cabbage and apples. Then there [were] the meat barrels and lard vessels and many other things in a well-stocked cellar. There was also a keg of kraut and a barrel of sorghum molasses.

When there was not enough room in the cellar they would bury such as potatoes and cabbage and even apples in long piles. They'd dig a shallow trench and fill it with straw, then fill the vegetables in that, then cover with clean straw again, then a lot of earth on that to keeping them from freezing. Sometimes when it was very cold they would pile corn fodder on the pile to keep it from freezing. The vegetables would come out fresh and crisp, the apples especially. But they were hard to get out when the ground was frozen hard. We would dig a hole in the pile and get what we wanted and then had to close it again to keep the cold out.

The kind of food fed to cows and chickens makes a lot of difference in the taste of butter and eggs, and even the flesh of chickens. I have never forgotten how when I was still at home our cows had gotten hold of some garlic in the pasture. The milk and cream and butter had the taste and we could not eat it or sell it. We all hated garlic. It happened in the spring that we moved and we had not learned just where the garlic grew. But when we found out where it grew we did not turn the cows in that pasture where they could eat it. And we did everything to get rid of it. I do think that we never were so near starving as we were that spring. We could not move as much food as we needed to tide us over until the new crop came in. Even the potatoes were scarce. Of course we had plenty [of] good smoked meat and lard and we had our chickens. But when our cows ate garlic, that was tragic. We were all fond of butter, but not when it had the taste of garlic.

Of course this situation did not last long, and with Mother's good management we got along until our garden stuff came in. At that [time] we could not go to the store and buy canned goods as now. We had to manage with the food we produced ourselves. But we survived and lived to laugh about it. We were a happy family there near the East Fork. The only drawback was that Mother was not very well. That worried us.

Another time we were visiting at my sister's in the country. This is more about food and the effect it has on the flesh of animals or fowls. The boys had cleaned the rubbish out of the garden and threw it over in a lane where the chickens could get at it. Among the rubbish [were] some old onion tops and some onions, too. The next day Sister dressed two of the chickens that had eaten some onions. She cooked them for dinner, but lo and behold they tasted of onions so strong that we could not eat the chicken. Some of us did not mind the flavor of onions in some food but we did not want it in our fried chicken. Both my boys hate onions. I think they inherited that from my father. We never dared put onions in his food. When Mother made potato salad she would keep a portion out for him without the onions.

Here is another instance of food flavoring. I did not taste this but I was told about it. A neighbor of my mother would do some trapping in the wintertime. One time he caught some skunks or pole cats as he called them. He skinned them and threw the carcasses where the chickens could get at them. For several days the eggs were so impregnated with the taste that [we] could not use them. That was even worse than the onions.

There [are] certain kinds of grass that the cows eat that give the butter an undesirable taste. We always liked what we called the clover taste. It always has seemed strange to me that the best tasting meat came from chickens and pigs, the two creatures that are the most repulsive in their eating habits. They will eat most anything. Chickens will eat the maggots out of dead animals or any offals of an animal.

I keep going back to horses. They were the best animals on a farm. It seems strange that so useful and intelligent an animal has become so useless, even on a farm. Of course, cows will always hold their own on account of their food value. It seems we could not carry on without them. Sheep are not so essential to our existence but they do furnish us with some meat and our woolens. But since then cotton and rayon have become so popular and [have] taken the place of wool to some extent. But we will always need wool for many purposes such as clothing and carpets and blankets, coats for men and women, and many other purposes, so it is still important that there are plenty of sheep on the farms. Pigs are also very useful for many purposes.

Dogs and cats

Here is something about our dogs and cats on the farm. We most always owned two dogs, a large watchdog and a smaller one that would catch rats and mice. We had one little brown dog named Topsy. She was a rat terrier and was very good in catching them. She had a litter of puppies and we wanted to raise two, one for ourselves and my sister wanted one, so we kept those two. Sister named theirs Carlo and ours was named Wolf, and the name seemed to fit him very well. Both dogs turned out badly. Carlo became a sheep killer and Wolf was just as bad, so both had to be destroyed. Wolf would watch the chickens when there was snow on the ground and they could not walk or get away very well. He would catch them and chew their feet off and leave them hopping around on the snow. So he had to be gotten rid of in a hurry.

But we also had some very good dogs. One was poor old Umo. We got him when a puppy when my oldest brother was a baby. That was before I was born. He was a very faithful dog, especially to my brother. Wherever Tony went, Umo was there, too. He was a very good watch dog, although not very big. I do not know what breed he was. He was a medium size brown dog with a white collar around his neck. We had him during the time they were building the Big Four railroad, and he proved a great protection to us. We called the railroad the three C's then—Cincinnati, Columbus, and Cleveland. Later it became the Big Four when they were working on it. It brought all kinds of workmen, some good and some not to be trusted. We were quite uneasy when our men folks had to be away from home for any length of time during the day or night. It was then that we were glad to have Umo around. He seemed to know that we depended on him to watch so nothing happened to us.

Some of the men knew and hated him. We were afraid that they would try to get rid of him. One dark rainy night father hadn't gotten home from town. We heard someone calling but Mother was afraid to open the door to see what the matter was. But she looked out and saw a man sitting on the high gate post, with Umo watching at the bottom of it. He had him treed, as we called it. We knew that father would soon be home so we let him sit there. He was not a bad man but just had a little too much to drink and could not get along very well. If we had known who it was we would have called the dog off. When Father came home he helped the man get down and set him on his way home.

There was a saloon in the village, and the men would go through our barnyard for a short cut to get there. Some on their way back were not very good on their legs and could make it no farther than our barn. They would crawl under the barn and go to sleep until they sobered up. Of course that kept Umo uneasy. We could always tell when any of them were around. Those were adventuresome times for [us] children.

[The men] made traps or deadfalls and caught small animals. Some among them were hen house raiders such as raccoons, skunks, weasels or occasionally a mink, and groundhogs or woodchucks. Some since we found out were harmless. We heard of a few foxes around and we knew that they were raiders. I have never forgotten how Tony teased me about seeing a fox. He even drew a picture of me trying to kick it. I had seen a dog that I thought looked like a fox and went home all excited and told them that I had seen a fox. But it proved to be just a dog and perhaps a sheep killer. They were common in those days. Dogs in those days could do much damage to a flock of sheep. Besides killing some, they would injure some so they would have to be killed and the rest of the flock would be so nervous and would lose their lambs. So there was no mercy shown to a sheep-killing dog, for after they had started that there was no breaking them of the habit.

Sometimes one dog would collect a lot of other dogs and they would go in lots. So you see what [that] did to a flock of nervous sheep. They were too scared to try to fight off a dog. It seems to be natural for a sheep to be afraid of a dog unless it is a regular trained dog to guard them. That way they soon learn what is expected of them and respect the dog and learn that it is there to guard over them and keep them safe from mongrels or killers. A good sheep dog is a great help for that purpose.

Dogs have been known to attack hogs when there are no sheep around. Brother Tony had one such experience. A dog had attacked a fine hog that he had for breeding purposes. A neighbor's dog ruined one of his fine hogs that was valuable, so it had to be destroyed. The dog was owned by people that kept more dogs than they were able to feed. So they were hunting for food. Tony caught them at it and knew the leader of them. He came home and got the old musket and went for the dog. He was very angry, and regardless of the people that owned it. He crawled under their porch and shot the dog. We shuddered to think what might have happened to him. He was beside himself with grief and anger, so he was not going to let it happen again. The woman was very angry and would not believe that it was their dog that did it. But the evidence was all there, so they could do nothing about it.

In those days we could collect a bounty for animals killed by dogs as there were not dog taxes then. The only thing was take the law in your own hands. I think the owner should be held for the damage done by their dogs. But the trouble usually [is] that the owners of such dogs do not have the good breed of dogs and do not train them right or they are not able to feed them properly so the poor dogs are hungry. I have known such families that had so many children and dogs that neither were fed properly. So neither turned out [to be] good citizens or dogs.

The dog tax law is a good law but the trouble [is] they do not get all the dogs. Some people do all they can to evade the law. They do not cooperate, so it is hard to enforce. We find it so here in the city. Many people even in the city these days think their dog has the right to anyone's yard [where] it chooses to roam or ruin and we must say nothing about it. I like a good, well-trained dog as well as anyone but it should be kept out of a yard where it can damage other people's property. There is no better companion or protector than a nice well-trained dog. But one that is allowed to run around and is not trained to obey can be very disagreeable and destructive. And the owner is the one to blame and should pay for the damage they do to property. We have such neighbors and they get angry if anything is done about keeping the dog out of the yard, even if it does not hurt the dog. I do not think the poor dog is to blame, and it should not be made to suffer for the fault and neglect of its owner.

A good dog can be trained so easily. They are intelligent and understanding and can be a pleasure and protection for more than their owners. I have known such dogs and they were fine to have around. We know such a dog that protects not alone its own yard but the neighbor's also. Such a dog is never hated and is valuable to have around. They can be so understanding. [But] I often wish something could take the place of so many useless dogs around. They are also faithful friends to have, but they can be such a nuisance and do much damage and are of little use where they do not have a place to rove around on their owner's property.

A dog [needs] a place where it has plenty of room to run around and a good warm place to sleep and it can be trained easily. I think a dog and a horse [are] the easiest animals to train to do the things we want them to do to become very useful anywhere. I cannot understand how anyone wants a dog without taking the trouble to make it a good and useful animal to have around. But most people that have a dog in the city depend on the neighbor's yard for a place to exercise and are very much offended if one objects to the damage it does to our flowers and grass. It seems to me it is about the same thing as taking what does not belong to one. The farmer does not let his cattle or sheep or hogs or even chickens run around on a neighbor's premises.

This is something I do not like to write or even think about. But such it was when one lived on a farm in a remote place some sixty or seventy years ago when there was something that had to be done. We had to do it regardless of how much we hated to do it, such as getting rid of sick animals or chickens or too many puppies or kittens. There were no SPCAs that we could call in to do these unpleasant things so we would have to do them ourselves. One time our little rat terrier dog had a litter of eleven puppies that had to be gotten rid of. The boys promised to do that. But Mother saw that they were waiting too long and did not want them to be any older so she had to do it herself. We would drown the kittens. But Mother took the newborn puppies and threw them on their heads on a big stone that seemed the easiest way to get rid of them. It was very hard on Mother, but we simply could not have all these dogs around and the older they got, the harder it would be to destroy them, If little Topsy had not been such a good rat dog we would have gotten rid of her. We tried once to rear two of her puppies, but they turned out so badly that we never tried it again.

When we had a sick chicken we would take it on the wood pile and end it there. That was not so hard. We were used to killing chickens. If we wanted a chicken for dinner we would go out and catch one and cut its head off and dress it in a short time. That was something we did quite often. We could not depend on the men folks for such things. We did not enjoy doing it but it had to be done if we wanted chicken for dinner. Of course if a larger animal had to be killed we would not do that. There were sometimes horses or cows or dogs that had to be destroyed, and there was only one way to do it. After Tony was old enough to handle a gun he took care of such things. He became a very good shot with his heavy old musket. We girls learned to do some shooting with it too even if it did kick us over.

It seems like we always had too many cats around. Mother could not bear to see them hungry and they were a pest to have around waiting until the milking was done, so they would get their pan of milk. We would have one or two nice house cats. But the rest would stay at the barn. But even then there were too many of them around. One time we had one that we wanted very badly to get rid of it. It had become such a nuisance in the house. So Tony when we butchered took one of the bladders of the pig and blew it up and put it in some dry beans and dried it. He tied it to the cat's tail and it ran away. As it ran through the fence the string broke and left its torment behind but it kept on going and never came back. He realized what a cruel thing it was to do and I do not think he ever did such a thing again. But he shot many of them after that. That seemed the most humane way to get rid of them.

To this day I am not fond of cats. I realize that they can be nice pets, but they can also be a nuisance. Two of my girls are very fond of cats and own beautiful yellow Persians. One is now eleven years old and her kitten is nine. They are loved and well cared for. I do not like any kind of an animal in the house so we do not have a cat or dog. Mother thought that cats were not good for little children to play with. They have some of the diseases that children have and their fur is a good carrier. So she never liked for us to nurse the kittens. I for one never wanted to do that, although I did not object to having a nice cat around to catch mice. I thought that it was necessary to have them with the rest of the farm animals and fowls.

Photographs

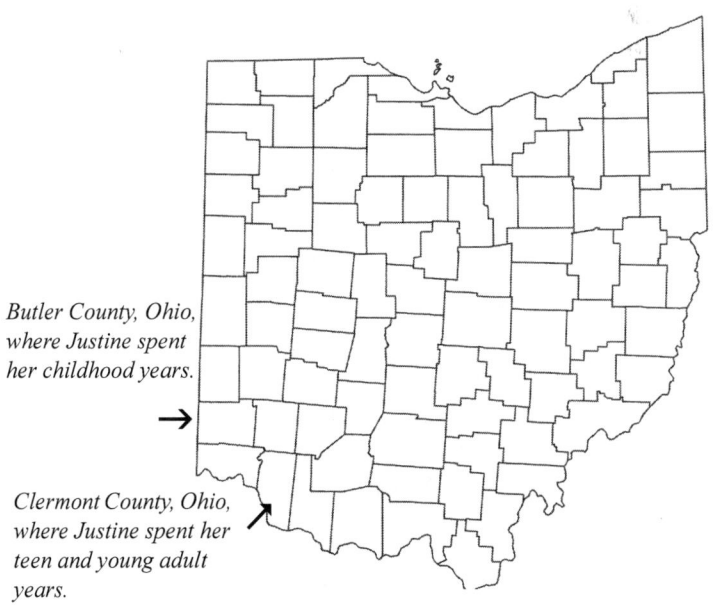

Butler County, Ohio,
where Justine spent
her childhood years.

→

Clermont County, Ohio,
where Justine spent her
teen and young adult
years.

Justine Klomann Hildebrandt's Matriline

Justine Klomann Hildebrandt
1861–1942

↓

Naomi May Hildebrandt Avey
1887–1936

↓

Margaret Hildebrandt Avey Walker
1922–2019

↓

Anne Elizabeth Walker
1954–

John and Justine Hildebrandt.

Justine Kloman Hildebrandt.

Daughter Naomi and mother Justine.

Justine with daughter Clara, and grandson.

Justine and sister Winona.

Naomi May Hildebrandt, age 2.

Naomi high school graduation photo.

Justine's daughters, Naomi and Clara.

Justine's daughters, Naomi and Clara.

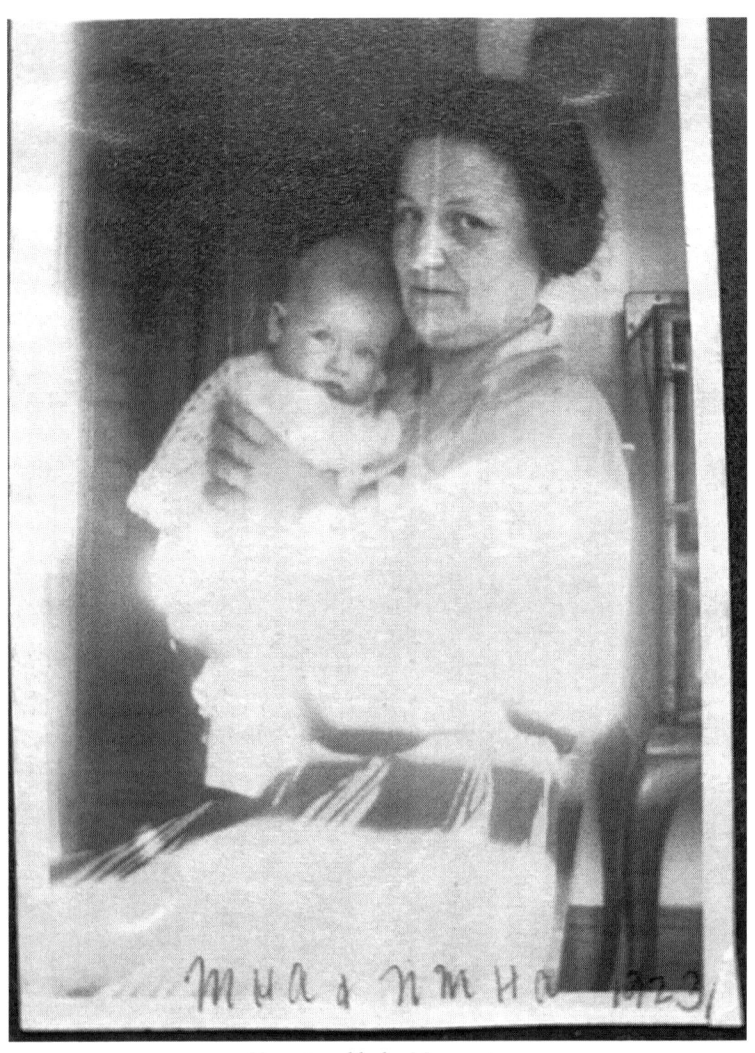

Naomi and baby Margaret.

Naomi, Margaret, and Albert Avey.

Naomi and baby Margaret, 1923.

Margaret (Peggy) and cousin Jim, 1926.

Margaret H. Walker, 1942.

Margaret with husband, Harvey Walker, and
children Anne, Carol, Steven, Ellen, and David.

Margaret, 1988.

Anne Walker, 1995.

Sister Ellen; Anne; niece Chloe; mother, Margaret; and sister Carol.

Anne and Margaret in Maine, 2009.

Anne and sons Zeke and Ira Pfeifer.

Four generations: Naomi and Margaret in the portrait;
Anne, Margaret, Chloe, and Carol on the couch.

Anne delivering Justine's manuscript to Cincinnati Museum Archives, 2015.

Button Charm String
(from website Allies's Adornments, http://www.alliesadornments.com/)

A charm string or memory string was a nineteenth-century pastime which consisted of collecting buttons and other small mementos and stringing them together. Young women of the 1860s–1900s would have parties in which they would exchange buttons and stories associated with them. Rules dictated that buttons couldn't be purchased for the collection and had to be gifts from other collectors, suitors, friends, or family. The gift of a button was considered lucky and the stringing of the buttons on a string enhanced good luck.

Justine's father's fireplace tongs.

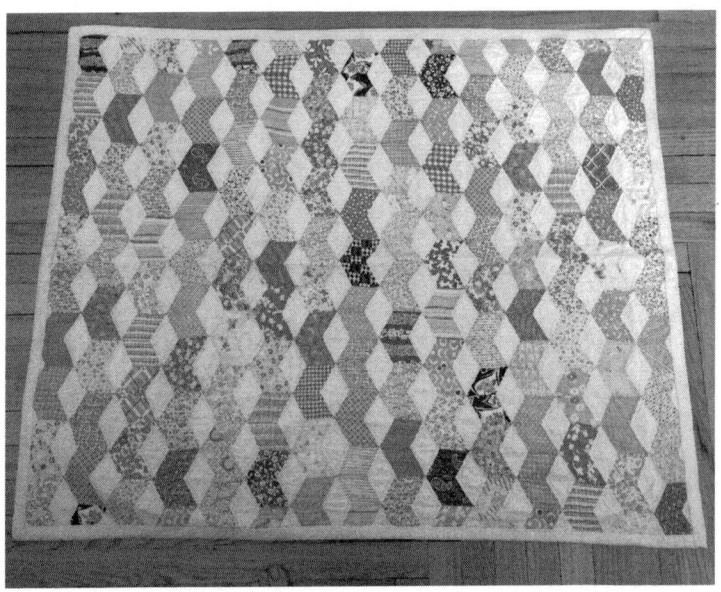

Quilt Justine made for granddaughter Margaret.

Rules for Students
1872

1. Respect your schoolmaster. Obey him and accept his punishments.
2. Do not call your classmates names or fight with them. Love and help each other.
3. Never make noises or disturb your neighbors as they work.
4. Be silent during classes. Do not talk unless it is absolutely necessary.
5. Do not leave your seat without permission.
6. No more than one student at a time may go to the washroom.
7. At the end of class, wash your hands and face. Wash your feet if they are bare.
8. Bring firewood into the classroom for the stove whenever the teacher tells you to do this chore.
9. Go quietly in and out of the classroom.
10. If the master calls your name after class, straighten the benches and tables. Sweep the room, dust, and leave everything tidy.

Typical one-room schoolhouse rules from
Red Mill Museum Village in Clinton, New Jersey.

Old Yard section, West Chester Cemetery, Ohio.

Justine's parents' grave, West Chester Cemetery, Ohio.

Justine K. Hildebrandt headstone.

Naomi Hildebrandt Avey headstone.

Chapter IV

Stories of Farm Life

Childhood pleasures and dangers

IN THE LOFT OF THE WASH HOUSE, a building to keep everything in, it seems to me we children would store our popcorn and walnuts and butter nuts and hickory nuts when we could find any. They were scarce where we lived. We played up there on rainy days. Some of our play things were up there. We did not have very many outside of our pets and some things we made ourselves such as sleds and wagons to pull around when we were able to play out of doors. We were never overworked. But as we got old enough to do some work that was not too hard each one had their job. The younger ones carried in the kindling to start the fire in the cook stove and to fill the wood box with small sticks of wood to start quickly so breakfast was not delayed too long.

We were never lonely. We never had enough time to do the things we wanted to do. We would get our work done as fast as

we could so we had time to play. We liked the long summer evenings and would play as long as it was daylight, then get ready
for bed and sleep so as to be ready for a long day for work and
play. Some of our games were ball, marbles, and horseshoe
pitching. We girls joined with the boys in these games. Some of
the ball games were four-cornered cat and town ball. Then there
were many more games we played: high spy and catcher and
races and jumping to see how high we could jump. We would
drive two stakes in the ground and lay a crosspiece and raise it a
little each time we succeeded in jumping over it. That way we
could see how we were improving. My father joined us in our
games when he was not too tired. He taught us how to run and
jump. He was good at that so we had many races. Other games
for the younger children [were] ring around the rosy and Black
man and under the mulberry bush and many other games for all
of us. We were a very healthy family and scarcely ever had a
doctor in the house.

[But] there are many dangers for children on a farm to be
exposed to. And I think now if we had realized what they were,
we would not have been so venturesome. One other thing that I
remember was when I went to bring the cows home from the
wood pasture. For some reason I went alone and it was getting
along toward sundown and I hoped that the cows were not too
far away, but I was disappointed they were not in sight. And the
far corner of the woods was some distance from the barn, so I
had to hunt for them. We had no bell on the cows, as some
would have, so one would know where they are. We never liked
to hear that constant tinkling. And we thought how it must
annoy a cow to have it on her neck and have to hear it with
every move she made.

This time they had gotten done grazing and were lying
down at the farthest corner they could get to and chewing their

cud with the greatest contentment and not a thought of getting home to be milked. By the time I got them aroused and started home on the path they usually took, it was getting pretty dark and I was getting more nervous every step I took. The path was around the side of a hill, with low bushes on each side. I kept close to the cow in the rear, with a stout switch to hurry them on. All at once the rear cow brushed against a bush and it flew back and struck me across the face and blinded me for a while. But I soon got ahold of myself and went on the best I could, with my eye smarting. I was glad when I got in the lane leading to the barn. A cow is not hard to train to go along a path she gets used to, and there is usually a leader among them that is a little more intelligent than the rest that makes her the leader, and the rest are willing to follow where she leads.

On the top of the hill of the lane stood a huge oak tree some four or five feet in diameter. It stood there alone and it must have been almost a century old, a noble old tree that stood there so many years and had been struck by lightning more than once but had stood the blows. But this time a bolt of lightning shattered it in the twinkling of an eye. It was shattered from top to the bottom. The top and branches were scattered about and the huge trunk was so splintered that it needed scarcely any splitting when it was finally all taken down. This happened during a storm in the summertime when the men folks were too busy to do anything about removing it. It stood there like a ghost to remind us of the wonders of nature and to show us the power of the elements and of something that the human could not control.

Another time we saw the lightning strike one of the rods we had on our barns and houses in those days. They are little used now days and I wonder why. This time it struck the rod that went down in the ground where they threw out the waste of the horse stable. One of the cows was standing nearby but the bolt hit the rod and made a deep hole in the ground and did not strike the cow. But you should have seen her jump. We were watching the storm and saw it all. We did not have any too much faith in the lightning rods but that time they proved their usefulness by not setting the barn afire, which happens frequently in the country. Of course when it struck that close to us we would all feel somewhat shaken up.

There is always something so majestic about a thunderstorm. I love to watch the clouds roll and hear the thunder peal. I am glad that it does not frighten me. But of course I do not like to see the destruction it can do. Here where I live now I can see where the lightning has struck some of the fine old trees. Some of them have been removed and made into firewood. When they cut up the old oak tree it made very good firewood, but it cracked so and threw out sparks and coals that we could not burn it in our fireplace. But it was good in the cook stove where it was kept under control and could not pop out. Mother always liked a good, sound dry wood to do her baking. Oak wood is very good to burn, but one objection is its popping. It has to be watched constantly so the fire does no damage. We never had a fire with all our open fires and I never heard of very many fires while I lived there in the country.

This is some more about our good times. I think that we were too daring or thoughtless sometimes. And I think something must have been watching over us so nothing serious happened to injure us. Of all the daring things we did, none of us ever had a broken bone. One thing was a grapevine swing that Tony discovered and tested. It grew on a very high tree, that is, it had run almost to the top of the tree and was very strong. The tree grew on a high bank along the creek. So Tony cut it so we could hold on tight, but nothing to keep us from letting go and getting a terrible fall. We would take hold of the end and by running back as far as it would go, then jump to give it enough momentum to swing clear across the creek and back again.

One time [there was] a neighbor girl no older than us. We were fifteen but she was much heavier, and not as strong as I was. We persuaded her to try the swing. She hesitated but we insisted until she took hold and swung across. But she had no good start and was slow in getting back. She got back on the edge and we caught her in a fainting condition. Of course we were frightened and never let it happen again. When I think what might have happened it makes me think how thoughtless a bunch of youngsters can be. Of course our mother could not watch us all the time so we ran wild sometimes. But the old grapevine was fun as many other daring things we did was.

One other thing we did was climbing up in the hay mow and jumping on a bunch of straw on the barn floor. If the straw was not very thick we would get a terrible jar. Another thing was sliding down a new straw pile. We could hardly wait until the threshing was done to try it. The first few slides were not so good. It took several slides before the straw became patted down to make a good sliding track. Sometimes several of us would start, one behind the other closely, and land at the bottom on a pile with bumps and bruises. But we did not mind them very long.

Not far from where we lived they build a high trestle and we never rested until we went up to walk across it. We had seen some of the boys walk across it so sister and I thought we could do it if they could. So we started across but when we got half way across we got pretty dizzy so we got down and crawled the rest of the way. There was a creek running under it and that made it worse. We were afraid that the gravel train would be along and catch us on the bridge. At that time the ties were set far apart. We could hardly step that far. We never tried it again until they had put more ties on it. It was a good way to get across the creek when it was too high to cross otherwise. Later when we wanted to walk across we knew pretty well when the trains were due and kept off when there was danger.

Our schooling

We had difficulty with our schooling. The roads were bad in the wintertime and we were in the center of two school districts, so that made it over two miles to go at either place. To make the way shorter we would cut across the woods or a field that was better than the muddy roads. One difficulty was that our neighbor kept a very big billy goat so we had to watch out for him. If he spied us he would come for us and we were afraid of him. That made us keep close to a high rail fence where we could climb in a hurry when we saw him coming. I have never forgotten what a nuisance he was.

But we were fond of going to school. We had a nice schoolhouse and two good teachers. Our school rooms were divided by a partition so it could be raised when there was an entertainment that required more room. The little room, as we called it, was for the children from the ABC to the fourth grade. From the fourth to the sixth grade was for the more advanced pupils. We had a lady teacher for the little children, a man for the older pupils. It took a man to handle the older boys, for sometimes they would go to school until they were young men eighteen and twenty. The older boys would go in the wintertime when they were not so busy on the farm. Sometimes they would get pretty lively and make it hard for a teacher that was not much older than they were.

In those days the rod was used. You can imagine how a boy of that age would take it from one not much older or perhaps not as strong as he was. When a boy was due for a thrashing he was sent out for a bunch of switches. Sometimes the boy would select [and] cut a switch so it would break when it was used. But the teacher would be on to that and would send another boy that he could trust to get a good one. Then the punishment would be even more severe. Sometimes a punishment like that would cause a riot among the rest of the boys and it looked bad for a while for the teacher. That would frighten the younger children so that they would have to dismiss the school for that day or until the feud was settled. Sometimes the directors would have to take a hand in it to get it settled.

And if there were some big boys that were not in school and wanted a row they would watch for the teacher as he was on his way to or from school. If they caught him they would handle him very rough. The girls with the primary teacher usually took the teacher's part and would try to protect him. If one boy would be expelled, that would start a riot that was hard to handle. There was always a leader in this trouble that brought otherwise good boys in it. I knew several of the boys that I went to school with that became principals of a Cincinnati school and were very good men. They have passed on now.

One man I remember well was my teacher. He was very popular with most people. He became principal in Cincinnati and was well thought of. He has passed on many years ago. My youngest brother also became a teacher in later years. It was more difficult for a young man or woman to get an education than it was later. But the ambitious ones got there if they were willing to work for it. I remember the many good times when we were going to school even if it was hard going sometimes. My mother would pack our lunch in a small tin pail and tie the lid on so in case we fell down it would not spill out and we would have to do without.

My favorite studies were reading, defining, spelling, and

mental arithmetic. I did not like working problems. I had no trouble with multiplying but I did not like fractions. I had one teacher at that time that I did not like and I think he took all the knowledge I ever had for working any problem. I saw him punish my older brother unjustly and it made me very nervous and angry. To this day I do not think I have fully forgiven him. Anyway I have not forgotten the occasion. Such is a childish memory after about sixty-five years. Those memories seem to stay with us, especially the unpleasant ones. But I think with me the pleasant ones are the stronger. Anyway school days were happy days.

There still lingers in my memory some things that happened when I went to school. One term we had what seemed to us to be an old man, and he had a long gray beard. He got along very well with the small children. But the big boys or young men did not seem to respect him enough to get what they were there for. In those days when they wanted an education, they made an extra effort to get it and were willing to work for it. He did not seem to be able to teach them, so for the want of something better they would get into mischief.

One day when he had gone to his boarding place for lunch the boys decided to play a trick on him. So they took hold of the bell rope that hung in the vestibule and dared one to pull it. Some other boy slipped up and jerked it so that made the bell ring. Of course that brought the poor man over in a hurry. By that time we girls had skipped out across the street to the grocery where we knew the storekeeper. We did not want to be witnesses and have to tell on the boys. We knew that no one could make the boys tell on each other because they were all guilty. One of the other boys that was not mixed up in it told the man, whose name was Meyer. He said "Drive them out, Uncle Meyer, and make them stand the fire." I do not remember just what was done at the time. But when it went before the school board the teacher was dismissed and another teacher hired that year. We had three different teachers so our schooling did not amount to much that year. But the next [teacher] proved [to be] a very good man for the older pupils. He was a man that commanded the respect of all the pupils. They liked him and they felt that they were getting what they were coming to school for.

Most of the older boys became very fine men later in their lives. One among them was a young German man that had arrived in the country from Germany. He could scarcely speak any English and understood very little. But he was earnest and ambitious to learn our language and our ways here. I remember how good these big boys were to him and they tried to help him all they could. There [were] some among us that could help him and he sought those that knew some German. I was one of those but our neighbor girl knew more than I did so she was able to give him the information he sought. I do not remember or I do not think we knew at the time where he went from our school.

Another of the boys that I remember that grew up to be a fine man was a crippled boy. He was handicapped by being lame and had to walk with a crutch. But he recovered from most of his lameness and grew up to be a big man. I heard not many years ago that he was a successful man and a good citizen. It was gratifying to hear about these boys and that they became successful men, and I think they remembered their good teacher for the last few years in a country school. Several of them went to college to finish their education and become successful men in their different chosen positions or occupations. Of course there were also some bad boys among them. I shall not write much about them. But one especially was an annoyance to us girls. We never could trust him and he became that kind of a man, a tricky trader that always looked out for himself regardless of who he cheated or got the better of.

There were some very fine girls going to school at the same time. I met one not many years ago that like myself had grown old. We were glad to see each other after some sixty years. Her son had heard that I had gone to school with her and brought her to see me. She has since that time passed on. Another girl I have not forgotten. I had been given a pretty little ring that I was very proud of. This girl begged me to loan it to her to wear for a while. I let her have it but I watched closely to see if she had it on her finger. But one day it was not there so I went to her and demanded my ring. Imagine my surprise and grief when she told me that she had dropped it in a well. I first could not believe it and I heard from some of the other girls that it was not true, but that she had given it away. And imagine my surprise when I saw my ring on a boy's finger. I went to her about it again but she stoutly denied that it was my ring and the boy was not enough of a man to help me get my ring. And as there were other rings like it worn at the time, I never got my ring back. But I always looked on that girl as a cheat and a liar. And few others trusted her. They knew what kind of a girl she was.

I liked most of my teachers and got along very well in school. I could read when I was seven years old. But in those days the little children that started to school at six years old knew their ABC at least and could spell some words. One day I had gotten my mental arithmetic lesson and a girl that sat in the seat with me was very slow in learning and asked me to let her copy it from mine. Of course I would not let her. It was a table that the teacher put on the board without the answers. The book would be taken up and we would have to write the answers after copying the table. She called me a name, and after that all Creation could not make me help her.

Finally when our slates were ready to [be] taken up, she did not have hers done. The teacher knew that I could get mine so he asked me to help her. But I disobeyed and would not do it. Of course that merited punishment, and I was aware that I deserved it and expected it. So he did not go home for his lunch that noon and kept us both to settle it or until I did help her. But there I sat. Finally he told me to come up to him where he was sitting. I got up and walked up about half way the distance between him and my seat and stood there and would not budge an inch further. I saw him turn his head and smile. Then I was not a bit frightened. And believe it or not, I was not punished anymore that time but had to get a bad mark. But it was worth it.

This girl lived in the small town near the school and I lived in the country. The town girls always thought that they were a degree or two better than the country girls. But when it came to getting our lessons, we knew just as much and sometimes more than they did. This teacher was the doctor's son and a fine and kind gentleman. Later he became a principal in a Cincinnati school and was very popular. His son became an Episcopal minister and many years after that time I went to hear him give a talk at the Church of the Advent.

A very dear and sweet old lady of ninety that was my teacher and also brother Tony's is still living in the village where we went to school. She was always sweet and kind, and I have never forgotten her smiling face when she read a chapter in the Bible in the morning before we began our lessons. That was done in those days and it is too bad that it is not still done to begin the day in our schools. The children need it.

[There was] another teacher that we had when I had gotten in the big room, as we called it. I was then in the fourth reader. He had been in the war and lost a hand. He had a wooden hand and always wore a black kid glove on it and it looked a little stiff but as natural as it could be made to look. He was rather handicapped when a big boy needed a thrashing. But he managed it pretty well with his one hand. How we did hate to witness a whipping but we had to sit there and see it all. The teacher would keep swinging the switch and sometime would break several before the boy would show any sign that it was enough. I think it was as hard on the teacher as it was on the boy. But that was the way they punished the boys.

I do not remember ever seeing a girl whipped. There were other ways to punish them. One way to punish a little girl was to stand her up on a desk where all the rest could see what a naughty girl she was. Or she would be stood in a corner with her face to the wall. That was not quite so humiliating. There was only one teacher and that was the last one I went to school to. He was very dark and we called him Black Bill. He seemed to take more out of me than I got from his teaching, so I quit school and never went back again. I was fourteen and in the fifth year. Our readers only went as high as the fifth reader.

After that was history. We studied of course the three Rs and history, geography, spelling and grammar, and singing in the morning before lessons began. I liked that and can remember how I liked my old song book. It was called the *Forest Choir* and there were many pretty songs in it. I kept my old book for many years. I liked spelling, too, and I was pretty good at that. There was always a rivalry in who could stay at the head of the class the longest. If we could keep the place a week we would go to the foot again and work up. That meant a head mark. There were quite a few poor spellers and sometimes it would not take long to get back to the top again. There was one boy in the class that I had trouble with. It seemed to be he or I at the head most of the time.

One girl that still lingers in my memory was our minister's daughter [Nacky]. Her mother was also my Sunday school teacher. She was their only child and a beautiful girl. She was a few years younger than I. She was in the same room in school with me and we played together at recess time. She grew up to be a very attractive young woman when her knight came riding by with his saddle and spurs and high boots on a spirited horse that took the place of the automobile which we have these days. It was a whirlwind courtship and he carried her off. He was Edward Scripps of the *Cincinnati Penny Post*. I do not know how he first met her. I think the first time he saw her was in her father's church. But I am sure I do not know what he was doing there. We heard that when he saw her for the first time he said then and there that he was going to have her for his wife. He bought and remodeled a fine old place in West Chester and lived there part of the time and the rest of the time in California.

Nacky's mother and father lived there. So their family were partly brought up in Nacky's old home. But later they, with her parents, went to California to live permanently. Her parents came back after some years. But her father's church had been taken up by another minister. He organized a smaller church at Sharonville, then passed away in a few years, a very tired man. His wife lived for some years in her old home when she, too, passed away. Nacky and most of her family passed away in California. Scripps we heard died on his ship somewhere on the coast of Africa. He was not what Nacky's parents wanted her to have for a husband. But it was romantic. They claimed their residence in West Chester as their home so when he passed away the township got the inheritance taxes. He must have been a wealthy man. The township got quite a large sum of money with which they made some extensive improvements. The residence still stands there unoccupied, they say, and still furnished. The caretaker [is] the husband of another schoolmate who has passed away.

One by one my old school mates are passing on, and I am

left to write about them. I enjoy doing it. It takes me back for many years. I am living those days over again to some extent. Some years ago when I would go back to a funeral of a relative or good old friend it would take me back to our home church or to a little white-frame church in the country. It made me feel very near to God. It seemed so peaceful and quiet. And I love the little country churches and sometimes the churchyard connected with the church. It makes me sad but I am still fascinated with rambling around in a country churchyard. Some [had] passed on for many years before my time, but I knew some of their descendants, so that would bring them near to me. Many of my people lie in the cemetery in West Chester, my father and my mother and grandparents and many other near relatives. My husband and two daughters all lie there near each other. I have always been thankful that it can be so. I can visit them all at one place.

It seems to me so many are gone. I am one of the few left. But when we drive along those same roads in our fast cars it is indeed different than it was and a very great improvement. I am one of the old people that thinks the improvement is good. We simply could not live like we did sixty or seventy years ago. It does not seem so long ago when most of the country roads were mostly narrow mud roads and almost impassable in the wintertime, and if the ground was frozen it made them so rough that it was impossible to go any distance in comfort. I often wonder when I see horses riding in a truck if they do not feel humiliated. They look that way. The poor faithful beasts are disappearing. But they are saved from pulling loads that were too hard for them. So if they are not here they cannot suffer.

I was always fond of reading. From the time I was seven years old I would read any reading matter I could get hold of. But there was not a great deal of it. We had the county papers and the weekly *Enquirer*, which was a little too much for me until I was old enough to understand. I would go to Mother to explain, and sometime some things would be too hard for her to do that to one so young. We also had books for younger children. Aunt Maggie would bring Mother her reading matter when she was through with it. One paper was the *New York Ledger*, which of course was not for a young child to read. But I read it or some of it and got to understand some of it. It was stories, and very interesting ones. Mother did not have much time to read unless it was while she was nursing one of the babies. It seems we always had one that was too young to take care of itself.

I read my school books until I had most of them committed to memory, especially the poetry. I still remember many of them, and to this day I love them. They meant much to me. I collected many poems and made a scrap book of them. I never learned to write any. But Sister Emma has written many of them. Some of them have been published. She would think of something while she was working, such as churning or some other kind of work that did not need deep thinking. She would go immediately and write it down. She was encouraged to write when a well-known writer heard her recite one of her poems. She has not had those published so far. But she should. Father told us many of the old legends and we have never forgotten. Now when I hear some of the operas over the radio it brings back those memories of many years ago.

It is the same way with the old songs. Some are some that mother used to sing the babies to sleep by. I think some of the old songs are ruined for me by the way they sing them these days [in]1941. Only the words are the same. Even some of them are changed. Some of the songs of Civil War days still linger in my memory the way Mother sang them. Father had a good tenor voice and he loved to sing. He taught us some German songs that he knew and he would sing the hymns with us that we learned at our Sunday school and the church hymns also. We enjoyed them all. We tried to learn as many songs that came out and were new to us.

Our church life was also very pleasant, and to this day I thank my parents for the trouble they took to send us to Sunday school and church when we were old enough to understand. My mother would get four or five of [us] little children ready on Sunday afternoon. That was the time that we had our Sunday school. There were two churches in the village where we went, and our services were in the afternoon.

We had quite a distance to go, so when the way was dry we would cut across the field where we had a path. We had to be careful so the weeds along the path did not soil our clothes, especially our white stockings. We would walk straight, one behind the other so we did not come into close contact with the ragweeds. We also had to be careful when we climbed the fence. Sometimes our father would drive us there in the spring wagon. But we liked the walking when the weather was fit. The way took us by a small burying ground, a family plot. We knew most of the relatives of the people that were lying there. We would stop there to rest and read the names on the stones.

One sweet, kind lady had been buried there for a short time. We would linger and look at her grave. She was a very beautiful woman and a kind neighbor. She came and taught my mother how to can fruit. It was something new at that time to put up fruit in cans. I remember after that how many, many jars and cans my mother would put up when she could get the fruit. We children would go and pick the wild blackberries which were very good and we enjoyed them so much in the winter in pies and sauces and cobblers.

Other amusements

I have often longed to go back to see if the places have changed much or if I could recognize them after so many years. One place I would like to see again is a place along the creek that flowed through the wood on the farm. It was a blue clay or soapstone bank such as we see along the creeks at some places. We were very much interested in the stones that we found at that place. It seemed to be the only place we ever found that we found the trilobite and crinoid. My oldest brother had quite a collection of them. I heard some time ago that his widow had given them to someone to place on exhibition at Bethel, Ohio. Later I saw some of the same kind at OSU museum and some at the art museum in Cincinnati. The crinoids were rare and I never heard of more being found than the one I found at that place. Brother would buy them from the younger children for a few cents until he had quite a collection. I remember that I got angry at him after he had given me five cents for my crinoid. He said he would not take five dollars for it. I felt cheated. There were other men that came around to hunt for them or buy from those that had them. Sometimes when we were sent to bring the cows home we would linger too long at that place hunting for these treasures and it would make us late getting the cows home to be milked.

We also were interested in finding flints, arrowheads, and stone hammers and axes, relics of the times when the Indians were still around here. There [were] the brachiopods or owl heads that [were] not so rare. We found many of them. But we kept looking for the most perfect ones. Those were found along clay banks, too, either the yellow or blue clay. We would take blue clay, the softest we could, and mold it into pencils. We could use it for chalk or to write on our slates.

We found many things to interest us and kept busy most of

the time although there were no picture shows or automobiles or telephones. There would be a small show set up in a tent with a clown Punch and Judy show and a monkey or two and a faker selling his patent medicine. They were patronized by some.

We had all the amusements we had time for. There were spelling bees at the school house, lyceums, and revival meetings to go to. One of the young men would hitch up his team to a big wagon or bobsled if there was snow on the ground and gather up a load of young people and away we would go. They were exciting enough for us. Sometimes we were permitted to go to a dance given at one of the young people's houses.

Then there were the play or kissing parties we called them. Some thought that they were not as harmful as the dances, but Mother thought different. Dances were forbidden by most churches, especially the Methodist Church, which we were attending at that time, it being the nearest. We had been brought up in the Presbyterian [church]. They were not quite so much [against] dancing as the Methodists. These parties were usually given on Saturday night. But we would hurry away before twelve o'clock so we would not be caught dancing on Sunday. It was bad enough to be dancing at any time, much less on Sunday. After we had gone to such a party on Saturday night we would get up bright and early so as to get our work done and [get] ready to go to church and Sunday school. At that time we had a very strict, old Methodist minister that watched the young people and their amusements very closely. After we had been to a party we would be afraid that he would hear about it and we surely would get a calling down or worse, sometimes put out of the church, which indeed would be a disgrace. I think if we did that now, then there would be few young people in the church. We did not feel guilty but we did not want to be thought guilty.

The square dances were a lot of fun. There was always someone that had some kind of musical instrument that would play and call the set for us. It was usually a fiddle and played by ear. Most villages had a band of amateurs that would practice and have someone that knew music to teach them enough to know a little about it. In the wintertime when the roads were too bad to drive a wagon or buggy, we would walk. So if we wanted to go at night and when there was no moon to light our way, we would carry a lantern to show us the way to keep out of the mud and pick our way along the fence where there was not so much mud. We could not let anything like that keep us from going when there was anyplace we wanted to get to. If we had, there would be many times that we could not go.

Sometimes when we girls wanted to go somewhere and had no escort I would coax Tony to take me. He would make me promise that I would go home with him if he took me. He said that he did not come home without me. One night he took me to an entertainment at the schoolhouse. We were without a lantern and it was very dark. One of the young men offered or asked to see me home. But I wanted to be as good as my word so [I] refused and said that my brother would see me home. Then he offered us his lantern. We did not refuse that, and I said that we would send it back the next day. He said that we did not need to do that, that he would call for it. But Tony [saw] to getting it back before John had a chance to come for it.

But Tony liked John and I saw him many times after that. He later became my husband. We had many nice buggy and sled rides after that. A good horse and buggy in those days was what an automobile is these days. We would take long rides on Sunday evenings in the summertime and go to picnics on Saturdays. Someone would build a dance floor in the woods for young folks to dance. And there were the camp meetings and the basket picnics for folks to spend a day in the outdoors for a social time together.

We would go to the colored camp meetings. A lot of them would gather in a grove and hold their meeting. Some of them were serious and very nice. But some of the new converts would get very excited and shout and scream and seemed to get beyond control. And of course the excitement drew a crowd of white people for that.

One Sunday afternoon John and I were attending a colored camp meeting. The weather was very warm and a hard storm came up. The wind blew and the lightning and thunder was very sharp and the rain came down in torrents. But we were safe in our buggy with the curtains all drawn around to keep the rain out. But when some of the trees in the grove began falling around us we feared some might fall on us [and] crush the horse and buggy as well as ourselves. So we left there in spite of the storm. We thought we were safer on the road than in the woods. But when we were near my home we met a man coming very fast on one of Father's horses and he had Father's coat on. I recognized them and knew something must have happened at home.

Needless to say, it made me nervous until we found out this man that we met was the undertaker and we both knew him. When we got home we found that the brother of a good friend of mine, a girl of our set, had drowned near my home and they had found the body and [had] taken it to my home. So that was what we found when we got there. We all felt very sad about it. He was a fine boy sixteen years old. He had gone swimming and had gotten beyond his depth and could not swim very well. He had gotten in one of those places where there was a sudden step-off. There were many of those kinds of places in the East Fork, and they were dangerous for those that did not know them and were not good swimmers.

They had some difficulty in finding the body until someone thought of a man that was an expert diver and swimmer. He came at once and dived down and brought poor Alva up. Everyone was nervous for fear they would not find the body before the storm broke. But they were just in time. When we had a storm like that the creek would rise very fast, and if they had not gotten him before the flood came it would have been difficult to find the body at all. The East Fork would be a raging torrent when a sudden storm came up. We could see it coming in a very short time after the rain had stopped. There was an island in the front of our house and it would soon be covered, so that made the stream very wide. Another one of those dangerous places was above the mill dam. It was very deep and was what they called a sucking hole. Good sized trees would disappear when the flood was very bad. It was even dangerous in the summertime when the stream was low.

One evening after dark when it was warm, four of [us] girls, two of the miller's daughters, and sister and I, thought we would go wading. We knew where it was not safe. But we got a little daring and thought we would go as far as we could before we got beyond our depth. The miller got uneasy and soon we heard him calling to us to go no further. He had his lantern and showed us how near we were to the edge of the forbidden place.

The East Fork does not seem to me that it is as big as it was in my young days. But none of the streams through the country have as much water in them as they had in former days. They soon run out after a hard rain. It is too bad that the timber that grew along the hillsides has been cut down. It seems such a waste. The soil in the hillsides never produces more than two or three crops before it is all washed away and is useless for even pasture land. A few hard rains wash deep gullies on the hillsides and take all the water that should be kept in the soil. That is the cause of the streams drying up so fast. I can see the difference in some of the creeks that I knew that had water in them the year around.

We also had our Sunday school picnic every summer and many such gatherings. There also were the county fairs that we looked forward to for several days of pleasure in the late summer. We enjoyed these simple enjoyments as much as the young or old do [today's] more elaborate and exciting times. We always had a lot of company, being three of us old enough to have company that brought a lot of young people together, and we had many happy times.

Another happy time we had was on Christmas. [For] many months or even years we would have our Christmas tree selected. We would usually know a long time before which tree we would have for a Christmas tree, and if someone else did the same and we got left we would be very put out about it. One time we had selected a very pretty tree that was growing on our place but nearer to a neighbor's place so they were watching it, too, so they beat us to it and got our tree. Needless to say, we were very angry about it. But we did not have to do without our tree. We hunted another one.

Mother would buy for us sugar toys such as all kinds of animals we had at that time. They were very pretty and quite natural looking. Then there were strings of rock candy and bright berries that we found in the woods. We would even tie peanuts or anything that we thought belonged on a Christmas tree. We usually had one toy apiece and we were very happy with whatever we got, I think just as happy as the children are in these days with all their costly toys they have now [that] are soon broken up.

The old musket

I thought I had written all that I can remember. But so many things are coming out from where they were hidden. I will have to begin again. I will tell you when Tony bought his first gun. It was an old army musket. He bought it for one dollar from a man that had been in the army. And I know that old gun had never been given such a shining before. The brass on it shone like gold and the stock was varnished and rubbed until it shone. He would make his own bullets. He could also shoot shot in it. He became a good marksman and made very good use of it. He was only about fourteen years old and it was very heavy. But he managed it well even if he did get kicked over when the charge was a little heavy. We that were strong enough to hold it up would try to shoot too. I remember what a bruised shoulder and a jar I got from shooting. He would put a can on a fence post and show us how to shoot at it. I was not a very good shot.

With that heavy old gun Tony became such a good shot that he could be trusted to shoot the hogs or the beef when we butchered. It was easier that way than to have to knock them down with a hammer, [which] was the way they had of killing the animals to be butchered. When he shot the beef he had to be very sure that the first shot would kill it for if it did not and the animal got excited there would be trouble. I remember one time when he shot the beef I stood a distance from him where I could see. The animal was in a pen and did not know what was coming. Tony waited until the animal looked up then shot. It was a sure shot so there was no excitement and I was greatly relieved and so were all the rest. I think that we were more excited than he was. It was the first steer that he had shot. But he said that he knew that he could do it and had confidence. After that he was called on by some of the neighbors to render that service for them, too.

When he shot the hogs to be butchered he had to be very careful not to load his gun too heavy. If he did, the bullet [would] go through the head and into the shoulder and spoil a good part of the meat. I was expert at knowing just how much powder to put in his gun. Sometimes he would put in just enough for the bullet to go to the brain and he would pick the bullet out of the head with his pen knife and melt it over to be used again. Father was good at sticking the pig so it would bleed well so the meat would be just right. He also had to be careful not to stick too deep and the knife go any further than the heart. That all had to be [done] so quickly so everything was done to make good meat. So you see how efficient a farmer had to be in his many tasks. I realize how gruesome this all sounds. But so it had to be on a farm.

Brother Gus would beg to let him shoot too when he was hardly big enough to hold up the gun. One day he came all excited. He saw a rabbit sitting in a brier patch and begged so hard to let him shoot it. He had been out with Tony so knew how to handle a gun. Mother let him have it and told me to go with him. He shot the rabbit and was a very proud little boy. His face was scratched by the briers in going to get it. But he did not mind that. We went home, he carrying the rabbit and I the gun.

In those days we had not heard of the rabbit disease so we were not afraid to eat their flesh if they were not torn up by shooting them with a shot gun. The boys would see them sitting and would get their gun and shoot them in the head. They were much better eating that [way]. Sometimes when the snow was fresh and deep the boys would go hunting with a strong stick. They would track a rabbit and it would not be able to run or hop very fast in the deep snow. They would throw the stick and stun it so they could catch it, or sometimes it would be killed if it was hit at the right place, such as the head. They would bleed it at once, and after it was cleaned thoroughly and left to freeze awhile, it was then good eating, although some of us, I among them, never cared much about eating their flesh. It was too much like eating cat.

You will laugh at this, what happened one time. We had a small orchard near the house along the road that led to the mill. The trees were very large old trees and grew some fine apples. But they hung so high from the ground that they were hard to get, and if they fell on the ground they would be so bruised that they were almost worthless. So we would climb the trees with a bag slung across one shoulder and go after them. One day I was doing that when I heard a horse's hoofs clattering down the hill. Of course I did not want to be seen up in the apple tree but much less when I saw who it was coming down the hill on Prince. He was on his way with his bag of corn to the mill to have it ground for meal. That was the way we did, to have it fresh. A bag or a bushel of meal would last for some time. So I kept very quiet and he was not looking up in the apple tree to see if he could see me. But when he heard about it he regretted it very much that he did not. Of course Tony had to tell him about it. I surely was up a tree, as the expression goes.

The black woods

Not far from where we lived, there [were] dense woods with many tall trees and underbrush and briers. Along a deep ravine grew some fine large blackberries. We had heard many tales of happenings in the black woods, and of course it made us somewhat nervous to go there. But we knew that the berries were there and we wanted them. So Sister Lizzie and I steeled our courage and went for them. We would get up at the peep of dawn before the sun was up and go while the morning was cool. We would go where the berries grew the thickest. That was along a deep ravine with the bushes hanging down over it. We would be very quiet and we would not talk to each other before we were out of there. The berries were large and fine but hard to get to. But we got them. We would get as many as a bushel at one picking. After we had our pack full we would creep out of the woods as quietly as we could and get home, two very bedraggled and scratched and ragged girls. Mother would tell us to wash our hands and faces and go and lie down so we would be ready to help her can them in the afternoon. A few trips like that gave us all the berries we wanted.

We felt there was more than one danger in that wood. One was snakes. One time I was picking as fast as I could when two little beady black eyes in a green snake were staring at me only a few inches from where I was picking. Needless to say, I did not want any more berries that grew at that spot. It probably was harmless but I did not know it then. Green snakes were not so common anywhere around there and some very large black snakes were seen there, too, so we never knew when we might come in close contact with one of those. There were also other things we had heard about to make us nervous. But as I said we wanted the berries and got them.

Not far from there at the corner of the main road and the little road that went by our house and on down to the mill stood an old deserted house with weeds and briers all around it. The old well with its curb was still there. It had the name of being haunted. Of course, we did not believe in anything like that. Nevertheless the very thought of what we had heard that happened there made us jittery. This was the truth and had happened a short time before we moved to that place. So [it] was still fresh in the memory of the people around there. It was about the murder of a woman in that house, and her body thrown in the well. She was murdered by a demented man that was roaming around there. They caught him and were about to lynch him. But they were prevented from doing that due largely to what the doctor of that community said. He told them that they might as well hang his horse for the crime as to hang poor old Barney. But he was put where he could do no more harm. But of course we never knew but there might be more such as he hiding in the black woods.

Another place that made us nervous was a bridge on that road across the little creek. It was near the cemetery, and no house near a calling distance, and in a sharp bend in the road. That road led to the village store where we went for our groceries. Sometimes we would be detained at the store longer than we expected and it would be getting along towards dusk. It made us hurry in spite of the load we had to carry. We would go after supper in the cool of the evening after our work was done. I being the oldest and the strongest, it fell to my lot to do that. As much as we could, we would find the shortest way. That usually led through the woods. There were many acres of woods there at that time. Well, the old house is torn away. But I still remember how it looked and how many things happened there.

One Sunday evening a neighbor girl and I had taken a walk along the road and sat on a log near the road to rest. We were talking the way girls of our age will do about our interests and not thinking of ghosts or anything like them when all at once we heard a door slam and a scream. Needless to say, we ran for home. But we were afraid of being teased so [we] said little about [it]. To this day I do not know what made that door slam. There was no breeze that we noticed or anyone around. If there was, they surely succeeded in scaring us.

My two brothers had an experience there, too. They were sitting on that same log after dark and you know how dark it can get in the country when there is no moon. They said that an animal that looked like a large sheep came rushing up to them and disappeared so fast that they could tell little where it came from or disappeared to.

Whenever we drive along that road I can see what a change

some sixty years have brought. The old house is gone and the place is just another field. The black woods is also a field of productive soil. There is little woods left. There are still some of the houses in the community standing there that were there when we were young and lived there. Among them is our old home in Happy Hollow. But the old mill and the few houses that were near are gone. But the stony road and the spring [are] still there and may never change. The East Fork and its surrounding banks and rugged hills cannot change. I love to go back occasionally and see where I spent many happy days of my youth. And I shall write more about them as I recall them from my memory where they have been tucked away for so many years.

Local travel

Traveling in my young days was rather difficult. It would take most of a day to go forty miles by train and streetcar and dummy and horse and buggy. Our home was in a rather remote place to travel from if we wanted to go to the next county to where we had lived to visit our relative. Sister Clara still lived there and of course we visited as often as we could. When we went in the summertime we would drive. But in the winter time most of the roads were almost impassable so we would go by train, that is, part of the way. From home we would drive about five miles to get to the station and take the narrow gauge train to Carrel Street Station. From there we took the dummy to the East End Car barn, then sometimes changed horsecars to another horsecar and then on to the CHD Railroad Station.

At that time the three C's ran from that station as well the CHDR. When we went to visit Grandma we would go on the three C's. And if we wanted to visit Clara we took the CHD, which took us to a station near Hamilton. From either place it was about three miles to get to their home and if we could not tell them definitely when we expected to arrive that meant a long walk, and with our luggage and a long skirt to keep from becoming bedraggled was not so easy to do. But we were used to doing hard things, so we managed very well.

I remember one such trip that Father and I took one rainy winter day. We had gotten word by telegraph that Aunt Maggie had passed away and of course we felt that some of us must go. Mother was not very well and little sister Eva was still a baby. So Father and I went. We started out in the morning and missed [the] connection at the depot and had to take a later train, so there was no one at the station to meet us. It was dark and raining, and to make the way shorter we went through the woods. It was very dark and trees had blown down across the old path which made it hard going. But we knew every foot of the way and felt at home there. So we got there tired but safe. Of course we had to come back the same way.

I made that trip from the station near Hamilton alone one time and I needed all the courage I could muster. When I got to the depot a man that I think drove a cab (he had a long whip in his hand) came up to me and asked me where I wanted to go. I suspect he could see that I was a green, confused country girl. I told him where I wanted to go and he told me that train had been taken off but that he would take me where I wanted to go. I knew that he was not telling the truth about the train being taken off and I did not like his looks anyway. I had been told of the danger of going without knowing where they would take us, so I took the horsecar to Fountain Square and on to the car barn. There were two dummies running from there. One ran on up to the station and the other one turned and went on to Mt. Lookout.

Of course I took the wrong dummy. But I soon found out when it made the turn that I was on the wrong one so [I] got off and walked clear up to the station where I took the train. I surely was relieved when I got to the last stop on the train. John was there to meet me with good old Prince, and the buggy and took me home. But as the years went on, things improved and we made many trips after that. I was so worried and almost exhausted when I got to the station to take the train. I was afraid that I would miss that train and there would be no more trains before the next morning. I was wondering what I would do, and [was] relieved when I saw the train still standing there. I bought my ticket and hurried again to get on the train, the next to the last change for home.

Old houses and cemeteries

When I was a small child I would love to hunt around a place where an old house had been torn down and find pieces of bright colored dishes and occasionally a large copper cent piece or perhaps a piece of silver that had been lost for many years. One time I found a silver ring. I wore it for many years until it was worn through and I could not wear it any more. An old house always fascinates me. It seems so pathetic. It seems to invite me to come in. I never see one but what I want to go inside to see if there is anything left in it that could tell me of some of the events that [had] taken place in it, of the births, marriages and deaths. For there is no house that has stood for many years, that these events have not taken place in them. When I see the worn doorsteps, and wonder how many have passed in and out of the door, most of them gone to their last, long home, and of the glad and sad times that had taken place in them. There is something human about it. I never see one but I want to enter and see it within.

And still some seem to me could still be used to shelter someone that has no home. It does not seem right for a house to stand empty when it could be made useful. Such a one is the

Scripps home in West Chester. I knew that home when it was the parish home. It must be nearly a hundred years old. It has been there ever since I can remember and that is seventy-five years. And it always seemed like an old house. It has been vacant for many years. They tell me that the furniture is still in it. The trees in the front that have been planted since the first owners lived there have grown to their full growth and it is being used for a goat pasture. I often wonder what will eventually be done with it. One of the descendants of the first owner is still living in West Chester. She was my teacher when I went to school in the little building which has been turned into a Catholic church.

The Presbyterian church next to it is the same church that most of my mother's people belonged to. It is the same one that I attended when a child. We went there to Sunday school and later my brother was superintendent of the Sunday school for many years. He and three of my sisters were members there as long as they lived in that community. He and his wife and two boys lie in the cemetery not far from there. That is my old home and I expect to lie there with those near and dear to me that have passed on. I like to think that it is a permanent place and not likely to be disturbed at least for many years. It makes me sad when I see the little family plots scattered around the country. They are very old. I do not think it is being done now. It seems like in those times when the country was somewhat of a wilderness they did not think that those little family plots would ever be disturbed. But many have been completely obliterated by time and may never be disturbed. I would like to think so.

Then again some of the bodies or what was left of them have been removed to a more permanent place. I knew of such a one. It was on a farm next to the one we lived on. Some of the descendants that still lived in the neighborhood or on the same farm removed their dead to a permanent place. Others, whose nearest relatives have moved far away, have [been] completely forgotten [but] are still there. Some places where the railroads wanted the place to run their road through the graves would be taken some place else, no one knows where. Such a one was near Gano, and when the Big Four made a change they had to have the old cemetery. It was not only a family plot, but there were other graves there, but not enough to protest about it. So the bodies and stones that still were there were taken to West Chester where we have our plot, and given a more permanent place to rest. But it seems sad that they had to be disturbed. Those people probably thought that when they buried their dead, that they would never be disturbed. But such is progress.

Another small burying ground that I knew was very old and seemed to have been just for the neighborhood deads' last resting place. I had wanted to see it. My mother had told me about it and I had never seen it. After Mother passed away, Sister Emma came home from college to take care of Father and Eva, who was then too young to take the responsibility of caring for Father and herself. Sister Nona was a nurse at that time and busy at her work. She later became a doctor. When my children were small they would love to visit at Father's and the girls'. Sister Emma was lively and the children loved her. She would play with them and make their visits very pleasant. My oldest boy Carl has never forgotten it after all the years have passed since his childhood.

One day we asked Father to tell us where this place was. So Sister and I took the children and started out across the fields, and after climbing several fences and crossing several small streams, we found it. Of course, the fence that has enclosed it had disappeared and most of the stones had fallen down and were covered with grass and soil. But several were still left standing and we could still read the names on them. They were familiar names and that made it more interesting. Among the ones that [were] still standing was a white stone somewhat more prominent than the rest. It stood there straight and solid, as much as to defy the elements to move it from its place. The name on it was one that I had heard Mother speak of many times. There was a daughter buried near this stone that Mother had known when she was a child. She passed away and Mother told us that she got sick after eating stick candy. Mother never could bear seeing the stick candy that had yellow stripes. When she bought mixed stick candy for us she would see to it that there were no yellow striped sticks among it. She told us of the horrible death of this young girl. After she had been dead awhile they opened her casket and found that she had turned over and bitten her fingers and struggled. How horrible. But as there was no embalming in those days, at least not in the country, that is possible that she had not been dead when they placed her in her casket but just in a trance.

In that old burying ground there grew a very large apple tree that had grown to its full size in the [time] that the place had not been used as a graveyard. When we visited it the apples were ripe and the ground was covered and there were many still on the tree. They were lovely apples, but of course none of us felt like picking them up and I do not think anyone else did. But Sister Emma saw the funny side of it and began picking some up and repeating the lines of the game we played when we were children, "Old Pompy is dead and laid in his grave." Of course, we could not help laughing at seeing her acting it out. That happened many years ago and I suspect that the place is completely obliterated by this time and has been taken up as part of the adjoining field.

There are many like that scattered about the country. There

are still some lonely, single graves under some remote trees on a knoll. I cannot understand why anyone thought they would find a permanent resting place on a farm where it was sure to change hands sooner or later. But some people in those days were very much attached to their old homes and did not want to leave them, even after death. I think that it did not enter their minds that they would ever be disturbed. Some even put up what they thought would be a lasting monument and there they stand, lonely and alone.

It is the same with an old deserted burying ground. I love to wander around the graves, and it makes me feel nearer heaven in its quietness and peace and to feel that nothing can ever hurt again. To me it seems indeed God's acre. It seems so safe from all the turmoil we are going through at these times. I love to go and look at the place where I shall be some day. It seems to me that the times are moving so fast and things are being thrust upon us with no time to find out for ourselves what it is all about. But it must be as it should be or it would not be allowed to do so. It seems to me that it is a clearing-up time and that it will be a better world after all this turmoil is over. I am sure there is a place for everyone in this world that God has given us for our temporary home. It has so many beautiful things and we have everything that should make us happy if we could see it the way God meant it to be. It is a beautiful place to be. But oh how we do mess it up. We that live in this good America should be very grateful and help the unfortunate people all we can.

The aurora borealis

It must have been in the early seventies when I saw the first northern lights. I remember how it frightened me when our hired man came in and said that the world was coming to an end. I ran crying to my mother. But Father soon told us more about them and they were only interesting after that. I remember several I have seen, but none as clear as the first one I saw when a child and the next one was when I was married and just gone to housekeeping. We were sitting in the next room and it was dark in the kitchen. There was a crack under the back kitchen door and we saw streaks of colored lights streaming across the floor. We ran to the door to see what it was. The lights were very beautiful that time.

The next one was last week, September eighteenth [1941]. It was the most wonderful one I had ever seen. It lasted the longest and gave most people a chance to see it. I hear that there had been sun spots. I think they always mean something and I wondered what was in store for us, and I said that I hoped that we would not have hard storms. Being time for the equinox, I thought we could expect a storm. So it was soon on the way. I hear that it did much damage at some places. With so much trouble and sorrow and bloodshed going on in the world, even the heavens are stirred. I wonder where it will all end. The only thing we can do is trust in God and do all we can to help make it better. I wish we could be more united in our efforts to make it better and love our country more than some hate the president.

I remember my Grandmother telling about seeing a rain of stars when they were living in New Orleans. That is something none of us [has] ever seen. That must have been over a hundred years ago. There had been several interesting comets and eclipses. One eclipse I remember was when I was a small child. It was in harvest time. It began about four or five o'clock in the afternoon. The men folks were busy in the harvest field, and Mother was getting supper when it got dark enough to light the candles and the chickens went to roost, thinking that the daylight was over. It lasted quite awhile and hindered the men at work in the field.

Chapter V

The People in Our Lives

Men that worked for us

*H*ERE IS SOMETHING ABOUT THE MEN Father would hire to help do the work on the farm. In the spring there were young men and some not so young come around to hire out to work during the summer and fall. Sometimes they would want to hire out by the year and other times for a shorter time. They were mostly men that had no home of their own. Some would be that had just arrived from overseas. Among them were Germans and Irish and a very few English and some other nationalities. Those that father hired were mostly Germans. They seemed to seek a place to work where their language could be understood. Most of them could speak no English at all. But it was remarkable how soon they learned to speak and understand the English language. They would tell father how much we children helped them to do that.

One of them said that he could understand me very well, that I spoke so distinctly that he understood me better than any of the rest. Tony was a help to them. He could show them what and how to do the work and he could understand and talk German to them when it was necessary. Most of the men were good work men and soon learned our way. The German boys seemed to hunt the farms to work on. The Irish were better with the pick and shovel, and sought that kind of work. I knew of one Englishman. He did not work for us but we knew him. He was very queer about his eating. He would never have more than one kind of food on his plate at one time. He would take his meat and eat that, then his potatoes and so on, but never more than one thing on his plate at one time. Sometimes he would not get to eat all kinds of food that [were] on the table. He was a little red-haired man and kept pretty much to himself.

One we had was an elderly man and queer. He did not like children and grumbled a lot at anything that did not suit him. He seemed to want a lot of attention himself and was disagreeable to have around. But Father kept him. When they were hired for a certain length of time there was no firing them even if they were not what they should be.

Another was a husky German. He was rough and drank too much. Then on Monday morning after a weekend of drinking he would be ill-natured and abuse the horses. Mother would not stand for that a minute and if she saw him beat a horse he would hear from her and he knew it. One time he unhitched one of the horses and beat it with the single tree. He heard from mother that time. He would be so untruthful that we could never believe him even if it was true what he was telling. Truth itself is not believed from one who often has deceived. His name was Peter and when one of us were caught telling something doubtful we would be called Peter. When his time was up he was not rehired.

At the same time we had him we had another young boy that made what they called a half of a hand. Mother was afraid that Peter was not what a young boy should be with. We knew his father and we did not want Herman to learn bad habits while he was with us. Another was a young man just over from Switzerland. He was a fine boy and a good worker but his health was not very good. But he was gentle and kind and had few bad habits. He did not drink or use tobacco. That pleased Mother. She did not like tobacco smoke. Father did not use tobacco so the boys did not learn to use it. Tony took up the bad habit after he was thirty years old. Gus never used it.

This young man was so very homesick. When he got letters from home he would tell Mother about his mother and sister and younger brother. He did not spend any of his earnings. He saved it all and went back to Switzerland when his time was up. Father would get out of patience with him. He thought him too much of a baby. But Mother felt sorry for him because he was homesick. One time while he was working for us he was sent to town with a load of dressed pork. The pike was slippery and he was cold, so he got off the wagon and was walking at the side of the horses to guide them. He slipped and the wheel of the wagon went over his foot. He was laid up quite a while with that and we took care of him the best we could. Mother would bind up his hurt and he did appreciate that and showed it to all of us children.

He liked having us in his room and liked hearing us talk to him while he was laid up. He would open his trunk and show us some of the things he had brought over from his home. He dressed well and went to church on Sunday. He was a good boy to have around and could be trusted. After he went back to his home we had one letter from him and we often wondered how long he lived after returning to his own country. We thought that he had lung trouble and I think he feared it, too, so [he] was anxious to get back home while he was able to travel which was not as easy to do as at this time. We missed poor old Frank after he was gone.

Another man still I remember was poor old Jake. He was an old soldier and he had been in the neighborhood some time. He was still able to do good work on a farm. But he did drink a little too much. But that did not make him mean like it did some others we knew. He did not save his money but he knew that he could go to the soldiers' home and perhaps had a pension. I do not know what they did about that at that time. Another we had was old Lewis. He was old and not much use to us. But Father hired him to do odd jobs around and help to feed the stock. We did not have him long. We knew him sometime before he came to work for us but we did not know that he had bugs in his head and left us some. Mother was very much troubled about it and did all she could to rid us from them. I had such thick bushy hair and she wondered what she could do about it if I got them. But she did not have any trouble with me. They did not stay with me any time at all, and I was glad to part company with them. They would crawl out on my neck. You can imagine what a disgrace that was.

Mother was very careful with our wash cloths and towels and combs. She always kept them separate from the men's that worked for us. We had no bath tubs but we had soap and water with wash tubs kept clean. When father would hire a man, he judged them by their clothes. If they came clean and reasonably well dressed, that made an impression on him. He thought that any self-respecting man should have a second suit to dress up in. One other man that worked for us was a young man that we knew. His parents were nice people but the poor fellow had epilepsy. We did not know all about it but I can remember, although I was a small child. We heard him fall after he had gone up to his room. There he lay in a fit, as they called it. I followed Mother and Father upstairs and saw him. And I have never forgotten how awful he looked. I have seen several cases since that, but the first case seemed to be the one that left the most impression on me. We were constantly afraid it would happen again, so he was not with us long.

Another man we had hired was a huge, red-haired German. He was an old bachelor and did not like children. We children knew it, and it did not help matters as far as he was concerned. It was then that our French came in handy when we wanted to say something we did not want him to understand. He was a queer character. He would go for days without saying a word to anyone. And his big red head seemed to get bigger than ever and looked like it was ready to explode any time. Tony was very much of a tease and he could get away with it better than the rest of us. He would say something in French to make us laugh and then we would have to run so Nick would not see or hear us laugh at him. There would have been an explosion sure. Father had hired him for a year, so he was with us that long. He was a good worker. Later he bought himself a farm and lived all alone in a big white house. I do not remember when his end came.

One day poor old Jake, the old soldier I wrote about, was teasing me and he called me a spitfire. I took his old felt hat and threw it with all my might in his face. It struck him across the eyes and almost blinded him for several days. I was sorry. I did not mean to hurt him that bad. He did not hold it against me. I think he thought he deserved it. And I thought so, too, at that time.

There was a peddler that came around about every month or six weeks. We would buy goods from him. He was a Jew. There were many such in those days that went around the county peddling goods of various kinds. It was convenient for us to buy when we were so far from the stores. I know of several that started a store later and became quite wealthy. This one made himself a nuisance by coming late in the evening and would want to stay for the night. In those days we did not turn anyone away as there was no place but the farm houses for them to stay overnight.

Well, this man said something to me that I did not like. I called him a *pourri chien* [rotten or dirty dog]. He must have understood it, which I wanted him to. He went to Mother about it but I had been there before he got to Mother, so he got no sympathy from her. She told him that he deserved to be called that name. Another Jew peddler that came around sometimes would get to our home on Friday night and stay until Monday morning. He would mope around all day on Saturday until six o'clock in the evening and then his Sunday being over he would begin to swear and sing and do everything to break our Sabbath.

One man that was the last regular man we hired for a year or nine months of a year was a young man that came to work for us. He was a good worker and knew how to do his work well and became a fine farmer. He was with us quite a while and later married my oldest sister Clara. They were farmers and later bought a farm and improved it and brought up a family of seven fine children, three boys and four girls, that grew up to become good citizens. We enjoyed visiting them in later years. Their children and ours got along well together and always had a good time. They farmed in a big way and had much around to amuse youngsters.

We were all so glad when we were able to do our work ourselves. Of course, in harvest or some other times Father would hire a man by the day so they did not live with us. And there were always men around that were glad to get work a day now and then. So that way we had many different characters around us and we knew which ones were good workers. In all communities there were always some men that wanted to live without working. We had such where we lived. They would visit our corn cribs and hen houses at night. It was then a good watch dog came in [handy] to guard our property or at least give the alarm when such were around, and many of them were ungrateful even if we tried to help them in their poverty.

One time Mother heard that a mother was sick. She had several little children and we knew that they were not getting the proper food or care. One day Mother baked a nice chicken and made a lot of nice gravy and sent me down to take it to her while it was good and hot. The woman did not seem at all grateful for it. I do not know if she thought we were meddling with her affairs or that they had more chicken than anything else. Mother never sent any more chicken after that. But the children would come to our house quite often and seemed to look for something. Mother could not bear to think that they were hungry and could not get enough to eat so she would feed them. I do not know if the mother ever found out that they were given food.

One time when we were threshing our grain they came up to watch the threshing and of course came in when the men came to their dinner. So after the men were through Mother sat them down to the table and gave them a good feeding that time. But their mother found it out and said that they got sick eating so much trash. It was the same food that we all ate so I do not think it was the food unless they were not used to our kind of food that we all thrived on. But it must not [have] been the food they were accustomed to and it may not have been good for them.

One of the hired men was a deaf and dumb little man. He had a boat, and when we wanted to get across the creek we would get him to ferry us over. It was rather difficult to make him understand just what we wanted. But he got accustomed to [us] and knew pretty well what we wanted him to do. Most of the time the creek would be too deep to walk across even in the summer when we had little rain, and in the winter time there always was lots of water. It looks to me like the East Fork does not have nearly as much water in it as it did in former times. There have been a lot of trees that grew nearby, cut down and some of the hillsides cleared. That may be the reason for less water.

Ike Crum and other neighbors

We had a neighbor, an old man that lived alone in a cabin near where we lived. Father would hire him to do some work for us. He was not able to do hard work but there was some light work [such] as mowing weeds and cleaning up. He was very superstitious and also suspicious. One day he brought over some mushrooms and wanted mother to cook some for us to eat before he would eat them himself. He was not sure enough that they were all right and Mother was not either, so she would have nothing to do with them. So the mushrooms were not cooked.

He was an inventor but never had enough money to have his patents tried out properly. He invented what they called the Crum harrow. It was a very good harrow and a great improvement over the old three-cornered harrow the farmers were using. Some seventy years ago Father bought one from him which he had made himself and knew that it was a good harrow. But like so many times the right person did not reap the benefit of his patent. It was a harrow in three parts, the widest part in the middle and a wing at each side that folded over the middle part mounted on iron runners, so it was easy to move about. It did not have to be loaded on a wagon or sled to take it in the field where it was used. When we drive out in the country, we see that the farmers are still using the same kind of a harrow with very little improvement as far as I can see. Someone with more money than he had got the benefit of his invention. We heard that it was taken away from him by some unscrupulous person, so he got nothing for all his trouble. It grieved him greatly.

He was one of those that wore sulfur and asafetida around his person whenever he went to the city, so when the weather was warm or the room he was in was [warm], it was not a very pleasant place to be. He was very much afraid of all kinds of diseases and would not go where he thought there was danger.

When I was about twelve years old the girls had the fad of collecting buttons for what we called a charm string. And a charm string was not complete before it was as long as we were tall. So it took many buttons. The buttons had to have what we called an eye. No holes were allowed. And there was to be no two alike. There seemed [to be] a good assortment of eye buttons. But we all preferred glass buttons. Poor old Ike wanted to help me get my string completed and would get all the buttons he could for me. Some were off his old soldier coat. And when he had a chance to buy a few on a card he gave them to me. I could exchange with other girls that had more than one of a kind, so that helped me to complete my charm string. I still have some of the old buttons in my button box. But I let the children play with them and they got lost, as all fads do sooner or later. Another fad was to collect all colors of yarn, and knit a long string on a spool and sew it around and make a mat for a table to set the lamp on. We always found something to do and never had time enough.

This is something more that has come to my mind. There was an old Irishman that lived [as] a neighbor to us. He lived with his daughter and her family. He pastured his cow in our pasture and was to pay a small sum for it. He could not milk and his daughter could not leave her children to do it. So he would bring his bucket when it was our milking time and said that he would give me fifty cents a month if I would do it for him. I [was] then about twelve years old and could milk a cow very well. Lizzie was younger and did not do any of the milking. So when it came time to pay me he gave the money to Lizzie. To this day I do not know why he did that. Needless to say, it made me very angry and [I] did not want his money or milk his old cow either.

He owed Father some money for pasturing his cow so Father sent me to him to collect it. I have never forgotten when I went where he was hoeing his potatoes and told him what I had come for. He did not even look up from his work, but said in his Irish accent "I hain't got a red!" And I do not think father ever got it. He would not pay when he could get out of it. Brother Tony never got over teasing me about it and he did not lose the opportunity to use the expression wherever it fit in. So I heard it many times. I think Tony would have been a better collector than I was. He would have argued with him and let him know that he thought he should pay it. But I went home and told them what the old man said and got teased for it. His daughter was a very slovenly woman about her house and herself and children and none of we children would go in her house. Whenever we were careless about ourselves or our work we would be called Bridget. That was her name.

It would have been different if the old man had been poor, but he was not. He had more money than he needed, but he would not pay his debts if he could get out of it. I want to explain what he meant when he said a red to those that do not remember when we still had the Eagle or white penny. It was a penny that had some other metal besides copper in it. They were scarce but we would get one occasionally and we called them white pennies. The old fellow we knew had more white or green money than red. Of course there was not much silver at that time. Our small money consisted of what they called shinplasters or greenbacks. They were paper dimes and fifteen cents and twenty-five and fifty cents in paper money. There [was] also five-cent paper money. There were large copper cents and two-cent pieces, and three-cent pieces that were white like five-cent pieces. There were still some silver five- and three-cent pieces which were very small. When we got them we children would keep them for keepsakes. I had some a short time ago but I have given them away.

This was a neighborhood of mostly French people. Several families lived near Grandmother and they all talked French to each other so I heard little else but French when I was there. Among them was a family by the name of Jonte. Mr. Jonte was a fine old Frenchman. He had a cooper shop where he made barrels and kegs for those that bought them from him. One day he went to the woods to fell an oak tree. As you know, most barrels or kegs are made of oak. The tree fell and part of it struck and killed him. They found him near his tree that he had cut down. For some reason that I do not know, Mother took me with her to his funeral. I was quite small and I had never seen a corpse before. It made an impression on me that I have never forgotten. And I went to many funerals after that but I have never forgotten his calm, white face, a good little man. Later his daughter was my teacher and I liked her. Mother would have me invite her to our home to spend the night and I would sleep in the bed with her. I liked that, too.

Visitors

There were some people that we knew that lived in the city. They seemed to think that they could come and visit us without being invited. We did dread to see the old lady and some of her family driving up the lane. We knew what a pest she would be when we were all so busy with our own affairs without her coming around to bother us. She seemed to think country produce grew without any work. She would start loading up her wagon on anything she could find growing in the garden and if she thought we had something put up for winter use she would ask for that, such as preserves or jams. But that was a little more than Mother could endure so she did not get her crock of preserves as she called it in her broken German.

There were many men [with their] horses, mules and plows, and scrapers and wheelbarrows, pick and shovels [who came to work on the railroad]. Some men brought their families and built shanties for them to live in while the work was going on. There were no steam shovels or diggers in those days as far as I remember. Most of the work was done with blasting powder and men and horses and mules. It took quite a while before it was finished. They made some very deep cuts at some places and the rock had to be blasted out, which was dangerous for anyone around when it went off. It killed several of our cattle and sheep. Later it was still worse when the railroad was finished and [there was] no fence to keep the cattle out. They would stray on the track and get [stuck] fast between the ties and break a leg or get run over by the train. Those were exciting times for everyone. It also brought some very undesirable characters around.

One morning after we had our breakfast and the men folks had gone to the field to work, four very well dressed men came around and asked mother if she would give them breakfast. She was afraid to refuse them. She fried them a lot of our good smoked sausages and a large platter of fried eggs, and being short of bread she baked them biscuits and so gave them a good breakfast. They had told her when they asked for their breakfast that they would pay her for it. But when they had cleaned up all the food they told her that they would be back and pay her. But that was the last we saw of them. Mother was afraid that they would come back and was perfectly willing to do without their pay if they only stayed away. I shall never forget what a mean face one of them had. It was the face of a real crook. And to this day we never found out what they were doing around there.

Chapter VI

My Own Family

Our farm years

THIS BRINGS ME UP TO WHEN I WAS TWENTY YEARS OLD. After over two years or [so] of many good times together, John and I were married on a rainy winter day. Well, I remember how I worried about the weather that morning. It looked indeed gloomy, and the East Fork was blooming and the skies dark and dripping. But Father tried to cheer me by saying never mind, you know, that after rain is sunshine, and I think that was true. The next day the rain had turned to snow.

But first I must say something about our wedding. We were married at home in our parlor at just before noon. We had a nice little home wedding of some thirty guests, a few relatives and the rest dear friends. My own relatives lived in the next county and they could not come due to bad driving. We had a very nice dinner prepared by my mother and our help as far as we could. I remember our cake baking was not any too successful. But the woman, a friend, was at our home making my wedding dress. So she helped us out with our cake baking. She was very efficient in many ways besides her neat sewing.

In the evening the serenaders came. They consisted of men that were our friends. They had organized a band and could play their music quite well. Sister Lizzie's best friend was one of the boys of the band. We received many nice and useful gifts. Many of them were glass. And I remember that I felt a little offended when one of the band boys said be careful of the crockery when they became a little lively. I said, the idea of calling our fine presents crockery. Of course, he laughed about it. A crock in those days was what we strained our milk in to cool and raise the cream, so our presents were none of them, although we needed many of the crocks later, and [they] would not have been a bad present at that. But I did not want my presents called a milk crock. Of course there was other crockery that was not a milk crock. But we always associated a crock with our milk utensils. And I was sure that I would need other things besides milk utensils.

The next morning with snow on the ground—you perhaps remember the expression, *the next day it snowed*—well, they teased John with that expression. John had a good horse and buggy, so we bundled up and started on our little wedding trip. It was not a trip to Niagara Falls but about forty miles away to visit some of the relatives that could not come to our wedding. Among them was my grandmother. She was then living with my Aunt Sarah in her own house. Sarah had come back from their former home so, Grandma being left alone, they moved in her house and took care of her for a few years. We had a very enjoyable time. We were treated kindly and were given a warm welcome wherever we went. And it gave John an opportunity to get acquainted with my relatives, which he did and seemed favorably impressed with the most of them.

So after our visit was over we returned home and got ready to go to our own home. John was a farmer like most of my people were. The farm that we were to occupy was not quite ready for us, so I returned home and did a lot of sewing for myself and helped Mother with hers. That left Sister Lizzie the eldest at home. But she was married to Will in less than a year after John and I were. After Lizzie was married and gone to a home of her own, that left Sister Winona the eldest girl at home. So you see how Mother's family was dwindling. But there were still enough of a family to keep them all busy. Sister Nona being only fourteen, too much could not be expected of her.

John and I started our new home on a farm some seven miles from my old home. So we were not so far away but I could get home as often as I had time to go. We still had Prince and our buggy, so we had a good way to go whenever we had to go. I never drove him. He was a little hard for a woman to drive. He was somewhat nervous and touchy. But he was used to John, and when he knew where he was going he would go without driving. John would tell how he went to take him home on Sunday evening after he had been to see me, how Prince would take him when John was dozing. He would turn out of the way of another rig on the road and turn in the gate when he got home. But he never did so well when anyone else drove him. He was faithful and reliable as long as he was not jerked or scolded. He could not stand that. He was not used to punishment and needed none. John never ever scolded him.

We had another horse, a little black mare that I could drive. John had lost the match to Prince, another roan mare. She had broken her leg and had to be destroyed. Prince and Jenny made an odd-looking team when they were hitched up together. But they were both good horses wherever they were hitched and could be depended on. When John was quite young his sister lost her husband and left her with seven children, the eldest a girl thirteen years old. There were three boys and four girls. John was free and on his own, so he went to be with his sister to help her rear her children. They were on a farm, too. So he stayed with them until the eldest children were able to help take care of themselves. He stayed with them until we were married.

So his sister bought a house in the village, and she and the older girls did sewing. They had two sewing machines, and they did what they called shop work. It was men's jeans, trousers, and some vests. The oldest boy hired out and worked on a farm. The next boy, thirteen years [old], we took with us. He was old enough to help some with the farm work and it gave him work that he could do as there was nothing in the village where his mother lived, a short distance from where we lived. We clothed him and sent him to school. So you see I started out with a family.

We also had another, an old man, a lodge brother of John's who thought it was our duty to take care of [him] the rest of his life. He could do very little work and made himself a general nuisance to me. Whenever he had the chance he would come in the kitchen and watch everything I did, and thought it his duty to tell me how. He would give me all kinds of advice until it got on my nerves and I told John that I could not stand it. John said that I did not have to stand it. So he told poor old Jim that he would have to find a home elsewhere. He felt bitter towards me and I did feel sorry for him, but he was so disagreeable I could not put up with him. Later he went to the infirmary.

The year that I was married Mother intended to give me a dozen chickens to start with, but the cholera took most of them. But she gave me a nice old biddy hen, and with a few that we bought we had by autumn quite a nice start. The hen that

Mother gave me reared two dozen herself. Father gave me a pig and a cow. The pig later had nine little pigs so we had quite a lot of them with those that John owned. We had as many as we could take care [of]. Mother also gave me a bed and John's mother gave us one and John had his bed, so that was all the beds we needed. Most people in the country had a spare bed, so we had plenty of room for beds and we needed them, for we often had guests. In those days people that were your friends would come to visit without as much as letting you know they were coming. But they took what we had and seemed satisfied. We never tried to be what we were not. We gave the best we had and they were welcome whenever they came.

Straw and corn shucks were still being used for beds in the country. John had hauled a lot of corn fodder in the barn to be husked when the weather was too bad to work out of doors. So we had a lot of nice clean shucks. He helped me shred enough for two beds. They lasted longer than straw did but they did need a lot of stirring up to make a good bed. Later we bought mattresses and got rid of our shuck bed ticks. I liked them better.

In due time our little girl came, so I was doing pretty much the same thing I had done all my life, babies, cooking, baking, sewing and everything else in a busy farm house. I reared chickens [and] calves [and] made butter, a lot of it. We had four cows to milk, and that was all to be taken care of. I did not do all the milking but I helped when I could and John was busy with the crops to be planted and tended. I remember one cow that I would not milk. She was a kicker. She would wait until you were nearly done milking her, then promptly kick the bucket over. She seemed to know just when to do it. She would not do it when John was milking her but she knew that I did not like her and she took delight in doing it for me. Finally she kicked me in the knee and I never would milk her again. We got rid of her and I was not sorry to see her go.

We also reared a calf a fine big red bull that became so dangerous that it was not safe for anyone to go through the pasture at any time. I was in the orchard one evening and had not noticed that he was near. There was a fence around the orchard along the road near the barn, with just two rails, so any one could crawl under it. He came towards me and I ran for the fence, of course, and rolled under it and screamed. John was in the barn and must have known what was happening. He came with the pitchfork and jabbed it in the bull's neck where it would hurt but not kill him. But such a bellow I shall never forget. We soon got rid of him. He was too dangerous. They could not turn the horses in the pasture where he was. There was danger of him goring them. There was a nice berry patch that grew wild, and one day a girl came to pick some of the berries. He came after her so she dropped her pan and ran as fast as she could and never came back, even for her pan. The berries were safe from any one that knew the bull was anyway near.

When John sold him he had to take him about four miles away. And there was only one way to do it. No one could drive him, so John got him in the stable and clamped a heavy brass ring in his nose and fastened a strong hickory pole about ten feet long to guide him with, another man rode a horse to drive him, and John kept hold of the stick or pole, I called it. I was worried and glad when I too saw two tired men come back safely.

John's sister lived in the village near where we lived so the younger children came over quite often, and I liked having them. It was not much change from my life at home. His sister's home was a good home with four acres of ground for a pasture where she could keep a cow and chickens, and plant a good garden for their vegetables. John would help them get them planted and Henry, the boy that stayed with us, would go over when they needed his help. We would give them a dressed pork when we prepared our meat. They also had a small patch of basket willows on their place that brought a little cash, so they got along very well. All the children grew up and made homes of their own, as far as I know. The oldest boy and the youngest girl never married.

My life on the farm for the next five years was pretty much as it had been at home, so I will not go over all of it again. We lived on a rented farm and were not doing as well as we thought we should, so we moved to a farm near my old home again and nearer to my mother again. We moved in an old stone house which had been built in 1816. It had not been occupied for some time and was not in very good condition inside. But the walls were very good and it was put in condition for us to live in it, that is, part of it. There was a frame part of six rooms built to it, which made it a nine-room house. We did not need it all, so the four back rooms were left vacant. The stone part had been built very sturdy. They said that it was built Indian-proof. The walls were eighteen inches thick and just as good as ever.

Shortly after we had moved there, our little boy was born. I would make a bed for him in the daytime on the window sill, which was wide enough for a good bed for a baby. He would lie there and amuse himself, looking at the trees, and the sunshine was good for him. He grew so fast and was able to walk when he was nine months old and a very good and healthy little boy. The woodwork in the stone part was made of cherry wood, and the mantles over the huge fireplaces were so high that I could [not] reach to the top of them. In the cellar was a huge wine cask. It was large enough that a person of medium size could walk in it when it was lying on its side. It made me nervous. I always imagined there could be someone hiding in it. I do not know why it was left there. It had been used to store wine in, in former times. I cannot imagine how they could ever fill such a huge barrel or hogshead, I called it.

On the same farm there was another big house, in fact it was a mansion of nineteen rooms, built of brick and frame. I could not imagine how anyone in that wild country needed such houses, and we wondered how they ever got the material there to build them. Of course they could get the stone for the stone house in the East Fork, and there was plenty of fine stone to be had, but where did that fine woodwork come from? We were told that the brick in the big house was made on the place. But at that time there were many other things that could not be made in that region where there were no trains or even roads that were good enough to haul large loads.

We were told that the big house was built by two Methodist ministers that came from New Jersey and settled there. They were brothers. Their graves are there in an old Bethel Cemetery in an enclosure with tall monuments. But they do not tell us much about their lives. Some think that they came there as missionaries, but we do not know anything about that, either. They were bachelors, so [they] had no family that we heard about. We do not know about any records that have been kept, and of course there is no one left to tell about them. So to us it remains a mystery. Nearby was another old grist- and sawmill such as one near my old home, and a covered bridge across the East Fork. But the old mill has disappeared and the bridge has been replaced by a new steel structure, and the road leading past them has been improved, and the frame parts of both houses [have] been torn away.

But the old stone house stands there as sturdy as ever and the big house has been improved. The property has changed hands many times since I lived there. The old stone house looks much better than it did some sixty years ago. So well are the walls built, they look like they could [last] more than [an]other century. As we ride through the country and we can see some of the houses that were built so many years ago I wonder why they needed such fine houses when they were so hard to get to. The roads were so rough and sometimes almost impassable. And another thing, there were not so many people in the country, especially in a rough country like this. The land on the hills is not so productive and one wonders how [they] lived. But we all know that their living was more simple, and horses and oxen could do the work without so much expensive machinery.

It seems that the ghosts were still around in that community. One evening after dark, Henry was sent to the store and to get our mail. He would usually ride a horse when he went. One night he said that he saw a tall white figure walking beside him as he was riding along. Needless to say, that made him very nervous. But he did not want to say much about [it] for fear of being teased. But he said that he would get that ghost if he could. So the next time he went, unbeknownst to us, he put a pistol in his pocket and saw the ghost and shot at it, but he did not think that he hit him, as it disappeared as usual.

But in that community at that time there were some undesirable characters living that made their living without much labor. Such a one lived not far that we suspected of visiting hen roosts. We missed the man and heard that he was sick in bed. We never [saw] or heard of that ghost again. But the man was seen again but not as a ghost. We were glad that it was not more serious. But such is the way that most ghost stories turn out.

After living on that farm we moved again about fifteen miles near the city. The surrounding country was not as rough or interesting with its ghosts and other interesting things around there. The farm that we left bordered on the East Fork on three sides. It lay in Horseshoe Bend. And in the spring of the year fishing in the East Fork was very good. The boy would catch all or more fish that we wanted. They made themselves a boat and set a trot line and we had so many fish that I got tired of having to cook them or having them around. There were some fine bass, but mostly catfish. John was very fond of fish and liked fishing. There was also good hunting and trapping in the black woods. Henry's brother George would stay with us in the wintertime when he was not hired out. A man was usually hired out to do farm work for nine or ten months, so that left him without a job for two or three months of the wintertime. There being nothing for George to do in the village where his mother lived, he would be with us. The boys felt at home with John and we just could not refuse them when they wanted to be with us.

George was a real woodsman. He liked hunting and fishing and trapping. In fact, he would rather do that than anything else. It made it disagreeable for me, but I put up with it the best I could. One day he came home with nine skunk hides. He had caught the mother and eight full grown kittens under an old cabin floor in the woods. Just how he did it I never knew, but it was very disagreeable to have him or the hides around for a long time. He made good money that winter with his trapping, but I was glad when the season was over and I did not have him around with his animals. John did not care much for hunting but shot a rabbit occasionally, and he liked some fishing. But he was busy with his work on the farm, even in the wintertime.

We raised tobacco and that had to be stripped and bulked to get it ready for market. That work had to be done when the tobacco was *in case*, they called it. It had to be when it was damp so it would not break the leaves in handling it. I always hated [having] tobacco around, especially in raising it. It made so much work. Early in the spring there was burning the beds to get ready to plant the seed for plants. The beds had to be canvassed, and if the weed seeds had not been all killed by burning they would choke out the small delicate plants. And weeding a tobacco bed was no fun. Then about the middle of June there was the transplanting and later the hoeing and worming and suckering and topping. Then later if the frost did not come too early to spoil it, it would be ready to cut and string on sticks, and hung in a building to dry.

Then they were ready to strip it. They would take it down and lay it carefully on a pile so it would not dry out before they could get it in a bulk. It took a whole year to get a crop ready for market. And then if the price was low there was not much profit for all the work it took to produce it. But in spite of all the work it took to raise it, wherever a man had a rich piece of ground he would plant a patch of tobacco. I never wanted to touch it. We at home had not raised any. Our crops at home were mostly grain and hogs and cattle. One day John came in and told me that he had something for me and told me open my hand. He laid a big worm in it. It was a long time before I forgave him for that. He did love to tease and he knew how I hated tobacco worms. I never could get used to them and wondered how they could pick them with their bare hands. I often wonder now if they have not found a better way to raise tobacco now than they did some sixty years ago. I am sure they must have.

Everything else has improved greatly. Even farming is made much easier with all the conveniences they have and the good roads and fast cars and most everything that city people have. But with it all I never wanted to go back to the country to live. John always thought that someday we would go back. But I never longed for a country life again. After we moved on the next farm we lived there only one year. It was not a very productive farm and it took all we could make to live and pay the rent.

The crops that we had to sell were very cheap. We raised fine potatoes and had a fine orchard of very fine apples, and we also raised tomatoes. John would get a large load of such produce and take it to market and come back with about fifteen dollars. He would get one dollar [for] a barrel of potatoes, three bushels, about the same or less for apples, and twenty five cents a bushel for tomatoes, or even less than that if he hauled the tomatoes to the canneries. Then he would have to take a few bushels of potatoes and apples to fill up the barrels that had been shaken down in the hauling. The barrels had to be rounding full. It would take the best of a day to get the load ready and then he would start about midnight in order to get there for early market. And if he got back the next day at noon he did well. So you see how one had to work for a little pay.

I did well with my butter and eggs and chickens. We had a good milk cow and I had learned my mother's way of making butter. I had a good huckster who came for it and gave me a good price for it and wanted all that I could let him have. Some neighbors found out that I was getting more for my butter than they did and they did not like it. So he told me not to tell them what he paid me. He also brought us our groceries but gave the cash if I wanted it. We always fed our cows what we raised on the farm or occasionally some bran or middling in the wintertime when other food was scarce. Some of the neighbors would go to a brewery and get malt sprouts to feed to their cows. It made a lot of milk but the butter tasted rotten. We never would have the stuff around and our huckster knew it. He told me about it and told me what butter it made when fed to the cows.

This takes me back to the last place we lived in the country. As I said, we were not doing so well, so we decided to make a change. When we saw the neighbors' little children picking their way to keep out of the mud along the road to their school, we wondered if our little ones would have to do that, too. Our little girl would be ready to start in another year or two. It was then that we decided to go where they would have a better opportunity for an education than we had in the county. So John procured a position in the city and we made a sale and sold out all our farming equipment. The thing that we hated to give up was faithful old Prince, and Cherry, the cow, that had given so much good service.

Then there was our dog, a very beautiful collie I had bought as a puppy six weeks old, and trained him in the kind of a dog I wanted him to be. I did not let the boys train him for a hunting dog. They would have tried to, and [would have] spoiled a good watchdog and other service he could give if he was trained in the right way. I told them if they took him out to go hunting I would get rid of him [even] if I had to have him shot. So they did not try to make a hunting dog out of him. He was very intelligent and could easily be trained to do the things I wanted him to do such as keeping the chickens or pigs out of the yard where they would stray if they had the chance. He was worth a lot to me. He would watch the children when they were playing. If I had an errand a short distance to a neighbor's, I would close the gate so they could not get out of the yard and tell him to watch them. He would look at me with that intelligent look as much as to say "I understand and will do it." If we left the place for the day he would not leave the yard, and I think anyone would have had trouble to get away with anything. We had taught him never to follow. He seemed to understand that he was to stay at home and take care of things while we were gone.

He saved us many steps in the evening when he saw [us] get the buckets to milk the cows. He would run ahead of us and seem so glad that it was time for him to do his daily work. All we needed to do was to stand at the open gate and wait for him to bring the cows. He would never stop until he had every head rounded up and brought in. The cows seemed to know that they must obey him. So they started home when he got to them. One time when he was still a puppy and did not know yet how to dodge a kick from a cow when he nipped their heels, one of them kicked him and injured him. I thought sure he was hurt seriously. The blood ran out of his mouth. But we nursed him and gave him warm milk to drink so he got over it and was as good as ever. It did not spoil him or keep him from driving the cows home.

We could have sold him for a good price. But when we had to give him up we wanted to be sure that he would have a good home. We knew that we could not keep him in the city. He was used to a place to run around and we hardly ever let our dogs in the house. He had a bed on an enclosed back porch and in the barn, when it was too cold on the porch. Somehow I never thought that in the house was a place for a dog unless it was when I was alone with the little children late in the evening. He seemed to know that he was wanted then and it made him so happy. We gave him to my sister-in-law. We knew that she would do all she could to take the right care of him. But he was not the same dog for them. We think that he grieved for us and died a short time after we had moved. He was [always] so glad to see us. My sister-in-law said that he seemed to grieve himself to death. He was only three years old and could have had a long time to live. Poor Carlo.

The next thing we hated to give up was faithful old Prince, our horse. We did not sell him but gave him to Henry to drive at a wagon to do some kind of hauling. But he only lived a few months after we did not own him anymore. No one but John had ever driven him very much and he was a nervous horse and used to John's gentle ways. John never scolded, much less punished him. He did not need to. He did what was expected of him.

We hated to give up old Cherry, a cow that had served us so well. I thought of the many pounds of good butter I had churned from the cream she had given. The last year we owned her she had twin calves. At four weeks one weighed one hundred and thirty pounds and the other one hundred and thirty one pounds. That was a lot of veal to sell to the butcher. She was bought by a man in the village for a family cow. Poor old Cherry ended her days as just an old road cow. That was a cow that was pastured along the road and watched by children so she would not stray away.

There is still more to say about faithful old Prince. John and I needed some more furniture so we and John's niece drove to the nearest town to buy it. The river had been high, and it left backwater over the road that led us where we wanted to go. The weather had turned cold and froze ice on the water in the road. John did not think that the water in the road would be very deep and he did not think the ice would be too thick for the horses to break as they went through. But it proved different from what he thought it was. So we went. But when we were about half way over, the water was too deep for the horses to lift their feet high enough to break the ice so there we were stuck in the ice. We were afraid that the horses would get panicky and begin to struggle to get out. The road was narrow and there was danger of getting into the deep water or that the horses would get cramps in the cold water. John kept talking to Prince and coaxing him. He would turn his head to look at John and stood as patiently as he could until some men saw us and came to our rescue. They had a boat and broke the ice as they rowed towards us. So we got out without any more trouble.

By evening when we returned home, the ice had melted and the water had gone down. After we got out, John drove the horses as fast as he thought was good for them to warm them up. This girl that was with us cried and said, "Uncle John, let me get out and walk." As if she could walk in that cold water. She was teased many times for that. I suspect I was just as frightened as she was. But I knew there was nothing to do about it but sit still and wait until help came. There was no danger as long as the horses could be calmed.

Our move to Cincinnati

After all our farming equipment was disposed of, we moved on the first of February 1884, to the city. We had visited friends several times, so everything did not seem too new. We soon got used to living in a big city and most of our people were living in the county and we could visit as often as we could get away. And our friends and relatives could come and visit us. We then had two children, one four and a half, and a baby born in the stone house, age three.

Something more happened while we were living in the old stone house where our eldest son, Carl, was born. John had to be away over one night. That left me alone with Henry and the two small children. Carl was then not quite a year old. He took sick in the night with what I was afraid would be croup. Having seen my brother have it, it frightened me terribly. But there was nothing else for me to do but get to work the best I thought how. There was no doctor near and no one I could send in the night to find one. So I went to work and roasted a lot of onions in the hot ashes of the fireplace and made a poultice and put it on his chest as hot as he could bear it without burning him. He soon got better and went to sleep. But I think I was never so glad to see the daylight come as I was at that time. The next day he was much better and soon was all right again. But he always hated onions and I wondered if it was on account of that time. But he never had the croup again.

Then in May of that year a girl was born, and when she was six weeks old the children took the whooping cough. So it took most of the summer to get over that. But our little boy did not have it, and to this day has not had it. In two and a half years another little girl was born, so now we had four children. When the baby was five months old they took the measles and I had them with them. I was very sick with them and they left me weak [and] clung to me for a long time. But I took the children and went to Mother's for a few weeks and got over it and I was well and strong again. Our little boy did not take the measles. He had none of the children's diseases and to this day at fifty-seven years has had none of them. He has been where they were in the home a number of times. His own boy had them very bad and again he did not take them.

When Clara was eight years old, Mary Margaret was born, and in two and a half years later John Emerson was born. In the meantime our oldest girl, Mina passed away at twelve years old. That was three years before Mary was born. And again when Mary was six and Emerson four they had the whooping cough and later the measles. But Carl did not take them of all the times he had been exposed. He seems to be immune. He has always been healthy and strong. When we came to Cincinnati to live, we rented a five room house on Straffer Street, a short side street where there was not much danger for the small children. We had friendly neighbors and we did not get homesick for the country.

One of our close neighbors next door, and the houses were built on narrow lots so that made the houses very close together, was Mr. Peter Taft, an attorney and a son of Judge Alphonso Taft and a brother of Charles P. Taft of the *Time Star*. He was a very quiet man and did not have much to say to anyone and seemed to want to be left to himself. So we respected his wishes as far as we could. I cautioned the children not to do anything to annoy or disturb him. He seemed to be an invalid. And at time he looked very weak and sick. But he went to his office every day when he was able.

One evening when he was coming up the hill he had a hemorrhage of the lungs. John was coming up at the hill at the same time, so he assisted him to get home and did what he could to relieve him. He had a remedy which he took for such spells and did not want a doctor. He had a housekeeper that was not much better and had sick spells, too. So I would feel it my duty to be a good neighbor. I went in one morning to get his breakfast for him. I prepared it for him, but did not stay while he was eating. He always treated me with respect and seemed a very fine gentleman. But at the same time there was something strange about him. He did not mix with the neighbors.

One day I had borrowed a shovel from his housekeeper to do a little planting and had not returned it before he came home that evening. And when I saw him coming home with a small peach tree I knew he would need his shovel to plant it. So before I let him hunt for it I ran to the back fence which separated our yards, and gave him the shovel. I was so sorry that I had given him that trouble and told him so. He was very nice about it and told me that I could have it any time I needed it. But we bought ourselves a shovel. We had neglected keeping one, not thinking we would need one in a city.

He was a good neighbor and never complained about the children making a noise or annoying him in any way. So one day when he was not able to go to his office any more his father and brother came in a fine carriage and took him away. They came and thanked me very kindly for the little that we had done for him. I had hemmed some sheets for him and did a few other little things for him that a neighbor should do for anyone. He changed housekeepers several times, and when he would have a new one, he would tell them to come to me for anything they wanted to know. That is what they told me. He seemed to like John and treated him like a gentleman. He did not live long after he left his home near us.

The next neighbors we had in that house [were] a couple with a little boy that took the diphtheria and died. Of course that worried me having it so near my three little children. But they did not take it, although it was not given, and careful precaution [was taken] to prevent more cases. Our two little children born in the country had none of the children diseases. Not so our two little girls, one born named Naomi, two months after we came to the city. So our troubles and worries in that way began. But then they were through with them before they were old enough to start to school. Our children got along well in school and I am glad that we were able to help them get a fair education.

Other neighbors we had [included] our landlord. They were an elderly couple, and the wife's sister that owned the house. They were also very quiet English people. They were kind to us and never complained about the children. They would let our children go through their yard for a shortcut but cautioned them not to have other children with them. They did not want other children to get the habit, and I did not blame them for that and saw to it that their wishes were obeyed and that our children did not abuse their privileges or do anything to annoy them.

Our children were good about obeying, and were seldom punished severely. They did not need it and we could do more by talking to them in what we thought the right way. Sometimes that can be more severe for some than a whipping. I wonder sometimes if it is best for children to be allowed as many privileges in not respecting the rights of older persons. I never could endure insolence or disrespect in a child to an older person. I had always been friendly with their teachers and they never got in any kind of trouble, so we never had any complaints from that source. And to this day I blame the parents for some of the misdeeds of their children. To bring up children right it takes careful training.

After living on the hill in a rented house we had saved enough money to start building our own home down on the Avenue which was a half a block from where we were living. We were glad to move in our own home where we had more room. We then had four children. That was in April and the next November we lost our oldest daughter, then twelve years old and well along in school. She was a bright girl. It was indeed a sad blow to us. We buried her near my little brother that had passed away with much the same disease. My mother and grandparents and two aunts were buried on the same lot. That is the grandparent lot adjoined [to] Father's lot, so Mina was there with Mother and Ernest. John is there now, and there is a place waiting for me beside them. It seems good to me to know that there is a space for the last resting place for this body of mine.

Sometime after we had moved to the city, Father bought a farm back near Mother's old home where she had lived most of her life. She was glad to get back. But she did not regain her health and did not live many years after that. Grandmother and some of my aunts were still living there, so it seemed home to her. She passed away in her fifty-fourth year. Grandmother lived some years after then, then too passed away in her ninetieth year.

Sister still lived not far in the same county near Hamilton on a very fine farm, so we went there to visit in the summertime. Most of our relatives lived in the country, so we being able to go to the country made it so that we never quite became just city people. Our children when they fell out with each other would fling out "country jakes" and "gutter snipes." But as a rule they got along pretty well and had a good time together. We still have relatives living in that community, and the family holds a reunion every summer. But the near relatives are dwindling and when I go back each year that I am able to do so, many of the young people I do not know, and [I am] not living there, [so] I do not see then often enough to know them. The young people grow up so fast and marry strangers. It makes it seem like an entirely different family, especially since Brother and Sister have passed away. There is still an aunt aged ninety-one, my mother's only brother's widow, living, but she was not able to be there at the reunion last summer. She had always attended until last summer. But each time there are some missing, so soon it will be only distant relatives. If the younger generation [does] not keep up their interest in the family relationship, it will soon be no more. About the only time they will meet will be at a burial at the cemetery where many of them lie.

Here is something more that I remember. When Mina and Carl were four and two and a half years, they both had beautiful golden curls. It was thick and soft, and I was very proud of it. John bought me a good brush and I tried to take good care of it. One day as I stepped out of the front door I saw a little yellow ringlet lying there. I knew at once what had happened. I was grieved over it. Mina had gotten hold of the scissors and cut one side of her hair off and the top curl off of Carl's hair. So there was nothing else to do but shingle their hair. Their father did that. So that was the end of the pretty curls until they grew out again. I kept the curls until they grew up. We kept Carl's hair short hair after that, as we did not want to make a Fauntleroy out of him. Our children all had beautiful yellow curls when they were young, and I liked taking care of their hair.

Thanks to the Almighty

When we drive over the same roads that we did so many years ago it makes me wonder how different it is. In those days it took a half a day to get where we get in less than an hour with the good roads and our fast cars. Of course it is much better this way. But it makes one wonder sometimes if we are any more content or happier. But it does not shorten life as we know. People seem to be living a longer life than they did then. Science has done so much for the health of the individual. And it is getting more so as time goes on it seems. Our work is made easier with all the improvements to help make it so. But I think there are more responsibilities also to take our time and thoughts. I am not one to say that these are not better times. But I wonder sometimes if we are not rushing along too fast, and that it gets us into difficulties that are hard to cope with. But I think if we do all we can and trust to the Almighty, we will come through all right. He will not give us more than we can do.

There are still many events hidden away in my memory that have not come to my mind. There are some things that I know you would not believe, so I shall not write about them. But you know the truth is sometimes stranger than fiction. I am trying not to exaggerate about anything I am writing about, so do not hesitate to believe them. I may have made some mistakes, but they are as I remember them at this time. I sincerely wish I had begun to write when I was younger. But as long as my children were young and needed all my care, I thought only of my family and the present. Now I have time, time to live in the past, and the future here on earth cannot be very long. But I can still enjoy life here. God has given me much to live for, and I still enjoy my life here on earth, and if I am spared I hope to be of some use in my very pleasant home, and the blessing God in His goodness has given me.

Afterword

A Great-Granddaughter's Reflections

---

*H*OW I WOULD LOVE TO HAVE KNOWN my great-grandmother! I was captivated from the first page as I read her memoir on loose pages in her clear hand. I knew that my mother had loved her grandmother, but Justine never "came to life" in my mother's stories the way she did in her own voice. I wanted to publish this memoir for several reasons.

Justine uplifted me when I was down

Two thousand fourteen was a difficult year. I had had a health scare in 2013 and was radically changing my diet and habits in order to heal. My sister and I had just moved our ninety-year-old mother to an assisted living facility in South Carolina and were sadly clearing out her beloved farmhouse in Maine. My husband had retired from a forty-year teaching career and was miserable. Our younger son had returned from seven years in

Russia with his new wife and they were living with us while trying to get established in the United States. There were green card issues, job prospect issues, and a buzz of uncertainty throughout our too-small house.

In September 2014 I helped my son and his wife move to Florida, where my son had taken an internship on an organic farm. My beloved daughter-in-law tried to be stoic, but the move was challenging and I worried about her. When I returned to our now too-empty house I was depressed. My husband was restless and had begun looking for part-time teaching work, but nothing would materialize until the following summer.

One day in October I came upon Justine's memoir in its pink stationery box, which I had brought to my home from my mom's Maine farmhouse. I took the handwritten pages out and began to read. Her words transported me. I was filled with a feeling of hope I hadn't had in a long time. My worries faded as I traveled back in time into her nineteenth century tale.

Over the following months I transcribed the memoir into the computer, sometimes for hours a day. My husband proofread and edited it after I typed the verbatim, unpunctuated manuscript. It was as transfixing as a good novel, taking us out of our temporary woes and into a world far from our own.

Justine was all of our grandmothers

It's not so much that Justine was *my* great-grandmother, but that her life must have been similar to so many of our grandmothers. The vast majority of our ancestors were farmers and yet as I write this, less than 2 percent of Americans make their living from farming. So, we share a common past, but few of us feel a connection with that past. By now I have read other memoirs of nineteenth century American women and I have felt just as moved by their stories. They are all our grandmothers.

Growing and raising food connects us to all people

I love real food, whole food, food from the uncontaminated earth. We are what we eat, and so are our families. Throughout my busy thirty-year career outside the home, I was the primary cook in my household, but food was hastily gotten from the grocery store, not the farm. A big part of my recent recovery from illness was learning to cook fresh food from a local farm coop. Justine and her family were more closely connected to the earth than I will ever be, and it was fascinating to hear how that feels. Farmers are at the mercy of nature and weather in a way that I have never known, and everything they eat is from the labor of their own hands.

Today most Americans are citified, living in pre-fab houses and walking on cement sidewalks. Our bodies and minds are distanced from the earth. What have we lost? For one thing, the common sense to eat real food. The saying goes, "Only eat what your grandmother would recognize as food!" Cheese puffs? Frozen dinners? Hearing Justine talk about the preserving of food for the long winter and the children's eagerness to eat the tender green shoots in the spring was exhilarating. Would we suffer less from the modern diseases of affluence—diabetes, heart disease, cancer—if we ate better? How has our sense of earth-connection changed as Justine's—and so many other families—moved into the cities for work, for education, for a "better life" for their children? What was gained and what was lost?

We are all immigrants

America has a unique story in that we allowed, encouraged, and in some cases enslaved or indentured immigrants to make up a new nation. It has not been an easy melting pot, but there is an impressive story here. Where else in the world have so many religious and ethnic groups come together and over time, in a cauldron of human idealism and cruelty, forged a society based on laws and opportunity? Justine's stories about her immigrant ancestors will resonate with anyone who was told their own family's story.

Voices of women in history are rare

Over the past three hundred years American culture has evolved from mere survival to today's focus on personal introspection and self-fulfillment. Picture yourself a hundred and fifty years ago, living in a two-room cabin with a dirt or rough-slab floor, a woodstove, and pallets for beds. Picture the scant belongings you would have owned. Picture the daily round of hard work on the farm, tilling the land, growing the crops, cooking the food, cleaning the clothes, bearing and caring for the children. What would you have been thinking about? How similar and how different would your mental life be from that of women today? This fascinates me.

When I was thinking about publishing this memoir I contacted the Library of Congress to ask if they had many such accounts by rural American women in the nineteenth century. The librarian did some research for me and replied that such accounts are rare. Farm women who knew how to write seldom had the time to do it.

Most first-person accounts by women about daily life were articles published in magazines, which arose in the mid to late nineteenth century. These publications featured advice on gardening, house and farm work, and child-raising, but the articles are carefully edited, not spontaneous first-person accounts like Justine's.

I have now read over a dozen memoirs by nineteenth century women. Some are happy and some are very unhappy. Two of the women had abusive husbands at whose hands they suffered greatly. Trouble with alcohol, tragic pasts, and lack of job prospects all weighed particularly heavily on men of the day. These tales are painful to read and they place Justine's cheerful voice in stark relief.

I love her voice

Justine gives us glimpses into her world, her personality, her feelings. She seems to have had a happy family life. She takes the time to say so, describing her close family, her love and concern for her mother, her closeness with her brother, Tony, her affectionate admiration for her father. In keeping with the rural traditions of the day, she went to stay with her older sister when her first baby came since she had ample experience both with housekeeping and childcare. Later, she took care of—and/or substituted for—her mother as her mother's health failed. She worried aloud about her beloved mother.

But she is surprisingly mum about such momentous events as the death of a family member, the toll of war, and the stresses of daily life. One of her siblings died young and it was noted, but either stoically borne or simply not complained about. Keep working. Keep supporting the family you still have. Were women more robust back then? Or is it just Justine? Was their stoicism a result of the English puritanical influence or did they simply not dwell on their suffering as consciously as we do today? Compared to Justine I feel like a complaining ninny! Maybe we just have more free time to dwell on our troubles. I am inspired by Justine's voice. She reminds me to be strong and above all, grateful.

Her tale reminds us that individual women throughout history lived and struggled and thrived (or not) in a very heartfelt manner. And she obviously wrote her memoir for some audience, whether family or descendants or the wider public. I like to think she would be happy to know that her words have reached forward 150 years. And I will send them farther forward.

Justine lived on the cusp of the greatest changes in the history of humanity

My mother, Justine's granddaughter, lived from 1922 to 2019 and experienced the greatest technological and cultural changes ever known. But Justine (1861–1942) caught a glimpse of these impending changes and gave us that glimpse. And In contrast to so many older people she didn't bemoan the changes! She admired what was useful about them and mused about their ultimate impact on people. From the vantage point of her late seventies she celebrated the "old ways" and appreciated the new.

I hope you enjoyed Justine's story. I decided to publish her memoir because of its historical interest, but also because I wanted this extraordinary, ordinary woman to live on.

Index

About the Editor

*A*NNE WALKER is an anthropologist, an early pioneer with women in the manual trades, and a retired public health administrator. She has lived in Missouri, Oregon, France, Michigan, Washington, Maryland, and Panama, and now resides with her husband in Bethlehem, Pennsylvania. Anne is the great-granddaughter of Justine Klomann Hildebrandt.

Anne Walker with her grandson.